From Nika Hazelton's Kitchen

ALSO BY NIKA HAZELTON

REMINISCENCE AND RAVIOLI
THE ART OF CHEESE COOKERY
THE CONTINENTAL FLAVOR
THE ART OF DANISH COOKING
THE ART OF SCANDINAVIAN COOKING
THE SWISS COOKBOOK
THE BELGIAN COOKBOOK
CHOCOLATE!
EGGS!
STEWS!
HAMBURGER!
THE PICNIC BOOK
WHAT SHALL I COOK TODAY?
THE COOKING OF GERMANY (*Food of the World Series*)
RAGGEDY ANN AND ANDY'S COOKBOOK
AMERICAN WINES
I COOK AS I PLEASE
THE BEST OF ITALIAN COOKING
THE UNABRIDGED VEGETABLE COOKBOOK
THE REGIONAL ITALIAN KITCHEN
LA CUISINE BY R. OLIVIER (*translator and editor*)
THE RUSSIAN TEA ROOM COOKBOOK
NIKA HAZELTON'S PASTA COOKBOOK

From
Nika Hazelton's
Kitchen

Nika Hazelton

Viking

VIKING
Viking Penguin Inc., 40 West 23rd Street,
New York, New York 10010, U.S.A.
Penguin Books Ltd, Harmondsworth,
Middlesex, England
Penguin Books Australia Ltd, Ringwood,
Victoria, Australia
Penguin Books Canada Limited, 2801 John Street,
Markham, Ontario, Canada L3R 1B4
Penguin Books (N.Z.) Ltd, 182–190 Wairau Road,
Auckland 10, New Zealand

First published in 1985 by Viking Penguin Inc.
Published simultaneously in Canada

LIBRARY OF CONGRESS CATALOGING IN PUBLICATION DATA
Hazelton, Nika Standen.
  From Nika Hazelton's kitchen.
  Includes index.
  1. Cookery. I. Title.
TX715.H3957 1984   641.5   84-20926
ISBN 0-670-24042-7

Page 324 constitutes a continuation of this copyright page.

"Garden Vegetable Soup" appeared originally in *The New York Times*, and
"Spicy Moroccan Lamb Casserole" in *House and Garden*.

Printed in the United States of America

Set in Janson
Illustrations © Mary Mietzelfeld, 1985

For Richard Schoenfeldt, M.D.
Who gave me help and hope

Contents

From
Nika Hazelton's
Kitchen

Introduction

This book is a collection of favorite recipes I have cooked over the years because the people I cook them for, and I myself, like them. It is not a standard cookbook nor a teaching manual, but a very personal assembly of dishes that I make in a way that I have found is the most practical way for me.

I like simple food, made with the best ingredients available, cooked with care and as quickly as possible to taste as fresh as possible. I use freshly grated imported Parmesan cheese and the very finest Tuscan olive oil, though I fry with peanut oil. I use butter because it tastes better than margarine. I don't use much butter in the first place so that I don't have to worry about cholesterol. Since I don't like fatty or greasy foods, I always cut off all fat and skin from chickens except when I roast them. I cut all fat from meats and skim off all fat that surfaces in cooking. I cook fish and seafood with good quality wines and spirits to add to their usually rather feeble taste. Since I prefer food that tastes of itself rather than of condiments, I use few herbs and spices in my cooking. I especially dislike the flavor of too many herbs in one dish, and to my taste, I prefer to taste either basil *or* thyme *or* marjoram *or* sage *or* whatever in one dish rather than a combination of herbs. As for spices, I feel less rigid about combinations, liking to put ground mace, cardamom, and ginger into nondessert dishes; cardamom is especially good with veal. I like just a whiff of cinnamon and cloves, and prefer to cook with stick cinnamon rather than with the ground variety. Since herbs and spices deteriorate in less than six months, even when kept in a cool, dark closet, I buy only small jars and only the most frequently used ones. If I need, say, star anise for a dish I may make sometime, I buy it for the occasion because I don't see any reason to keep herbs and spices for "just in case I need them." I had a sad experience with juniper berries I had kept for so long that they had lost all flavor when I wanted to use them. I have great feelings about chili powder. Chili is not only a dish but is also a state of mind that excites the passions, and only the chili powder one loves will do. Better no chili than chili made with an alien powder. On the other hand, soy sauce is nice whether bought in a supermarket or health food store, and I find it a most useful seasoning for hamburger; just a splash over the raw meat and it will have some taste without fuss on the cook's part.

I make cakes the old-fashioned way—from scratch—and invariably use large eggs. I have a few excellent heavy restaurant aluminum saucepans and a few enamel-lined casseroles that can go to the table, along with white soufflé and au gratin dishes that I also use for serving dishes. I use a KitchenAid to mix, a Cuisinart to mince, a rotary peeler to peel, and a small mandolin to cut transparent slices of potatoes and cucumbers. My kitchen also sports a couple of balloon whisks, wooden spoons, good knives, and a very sharp pair of scissors, as well as the standard paraphernalia of measuring cups, mixing bowls, measuring spoons, and so forth. I eat from silver flatware and have done so even in my days of poverty when it was suggested to me to sell or pawn it to get some cash, and I don't mind using silver for cooking as well. My glasses are simple, inexpensive standard ten-ounce glasses which I use for wine and every kind of drink.

What staples do I keep? Stocking the larder depends on where you live, how many people you cook for, if you get many unannounced guests, and your cooking habits. If you are in the country and cook for many people, remember that it is not always possible to jump into the car and get some food (it may be snowing hard or the car may not work or you just cannot leave the house), so have enough stuff on hand to fix a meal. Your faithful standard cookbook will tell you how much and what to stock. Since I now live in the city and don't have much kitchen space, I keep the bare essentials on hand (I shop especially when I have company), such as pasta, rice, cream of wheat (for upset stomachs there is nothing like it when cooked just in water), and cornmeal. I use very few canned foods (tomatoes, chickpeas, and beans, the latter two in small cans for the two of us, my husband and myself). And talking of beans, baked ones I mean, I find that the brand that is baked without tomato sauce is quite as good as any home-baked beans; I have fooled the greatest Boston-baked-bean connoisseurs with them. I also stock crackers because we constantly run out of bread. (I don't bake any because why bake when I can buy wonderful bread since I live in New York City?) And of course, I always have hunks of *good* Parmesan and cheddar in the refrigerator for grating, eating, and cooking. The cooking applies to cheese soufflés, which I make when I can't think of anything else that is nice, substantial, and healthy.

When it comes to puff paste, you may wonder why I use the frozen patty shells available in supermarkets. Puff paste is a nuisance to make and not worth it unless you use a lot of it, and you'll find the basic puff paste recipe in any good standard cookbook. Since puff paste in sheets is not readily available, I buy the readily available frozen puff paste patty shells you can always find in the frozen food section; just roll them out according to the recipe.

As to wines and spirits for cooking, I use the ones we drink, and I am not above nipping myself (cooks will nip, alas) what I cook with. I must admit that both wines and spirits are better than average in our house because we both drink very little and for the flavor rather than for the effect. Nor do I use much wine or spirits in my cooking; I think that both can overpower the true flavor of a food.

From all of this, it is obvious that I like to keep things simple. I trust to have done so in this book, where I have expounded only when experience has proved to me that it was necessary, such as in the chapters on chicken and meat.

Possibly because I have had to cook for a family as well as professionally all my life, I take a somewhat dispassionate view of cooking. Cooking is largely a matter of practice and interest, and it is nonsense to say or to believe that you turn into what is loathsomely called a "gourmet cook" or that you master the art of cooking by following a recipe a few times. Be that as it may, I recommend that all human beings learn to prepare a few dishes so that he/she or she/he can put a meal together when needed, which is more often than you may think. If you have to cook every day, learn to do it as well as you possibly can. It is nice to be able to please others and oneself with one's skills. Besides, good cooks always have friends, and are seldom abandoned by their spouses or partners—if that is of any importance to you.

Before we get to the eternal question of what to cook, let me explain more fully my ways of cooking and the choice of wording in my recipes.

First of all, I would like to repeat that this is not a standard cookbook nor a teaching manual. The book takes for granted that you have cooked before; if not, I suggest that you learn from a cookbook for beginners. However, to alleviate any doubts as to what I mean to say in my recipes, here goes.

Almost all cooking, except baking, is a more-or-less process, where you adjust the ingredients and cooking times as you go along and utilize the cooking utensils you have at hand. When I suggest the size of a baking dish or any other utensil, I do so largely to give the cook an idea of how large a utensil he or she will need to accommodate the volume of the ingredients in the recipe for best results. It is frequently impossible to state the amount of liquid used in a recipe, (such as to cover meats or vegetables) since this depends on the size and shape of the utensil used as well as on the amount of sauce desired. It also depends on the way the dish will be served, that is, either in its own cooking vessel if it is one that can go to the table, or whether it will be transferred to a serving dish.

As to oven temperature, I have stuck to the tried and proven way of specifying that the oven should be slow, medium, or hot, followed by the specific temperature in degrees Fahrenheit. I know that people use ovens with no thermostatic control, or that the latter does not work properly, and since they may not own a portable oven thermometer, I know from many years of experience in the food world that they will want to know what kind of heat is wanted and how to get it in their ovens, provided it is spelled out in words rather than degrees Fahrenheit only. I also like to use the word "thoroughly" when, for instance, I say that a dish or food should be heated through, to remind the cook that a dish may be hot on its surface but not throughout. If advised "to heat through thoroughly" the cook will be reminded to pay attention to the temperature of the dish.

It has been brought to my attention that my readers may not know what I mean exactly when I use the terms "cool" or "chilled." Cool means that a dish is just that, no longer lukewarm from cooking, independently from the temperature of the kitchen or room where it stands, which may be very hot. Chilled means that a dish has been refrigerated or kept over ice until extremely cold, but neither icy nor frozen.

As any cook knows, the fat used to coat baking dishes or sheets affects the taste of the dish. I invariably, with excellent results, use butter to coat my cake pans and baking dishes, because I do not like the flavors of margarine, hydrogenated fats, cooking or salad oils, bacon grease, lard, or any other fat implied in the term "grease, etcetera." I know full well that butter will burn at high temperatures, on the stove or in the oven. But my recipes, all tried and proven over a period of many years, do not call for an exposure to heat for a length of time that may be detrimental to the heat tolerance of the butter. When I say "butter a dish, etcetera," I mean just that, just as when I use the words "grease, etcetera" a dish, I mean that you can use the grease of your choice, since you will know that the final flavor of what you are cooking or baking depends on the fats used in the recipe. Incidentally, any cook knows that the amount of butter or "grease" needed to prepare a baking dish is not part of the ingredients and need not be mentioned.

Other specific points are well known to the cook who has cooked before, though it might not be amiss to mention them here. I call my butter sweet rather than unsalted because that is to me the clearer way. But I, like all cooks, know that you can cook almost everything with either kind of butter without changing the flavor of a dish in an appreciable way. When the butter has to be one kind I am specific in calling for "sweet" butter as the case may be. The yogurt I use is always plain yogurt.

I also try to be consistent in telling cooks whether a dish should be cooked with or without a cover. True enough, this should be clear from the instructions given in the recipe, but since few of us have totally focused minds when reading a recipe, this extremely important cooking point may be overlooked. Besides, how many of us bother to read a recipe as accurately as a pharmacist reads a doctor's prescription? I for one frequently don't, to my later sorrow.

Since this is not a cookbook for beginners, I have not specified accurately the time when to start a recipe. From reading the recipe it becomes clear that it may have to be started a day (or more) ahead. I leave it to the cook to do this early cooking any way it fits in with the cook's plans and/or work. One well-known cook said to me, "I usually cook at midnight after everybody has gone to bed. Is that a day ahead?" Is it? I don't know.

I tried to be as accurate as possible when speaking of ingredients, bearing in mind that this is not a standard cookbook nor a teaching manual. A cook would know that the size of a carrot in soup or stew is not of the utmost importance, since carrots do not vary greatly in size; that potatoes, carrots, garlic, and onions are peeled unless the recipe says otherwise; that tomatoes can be peeled and/or seeded depending on how the cook feels at the moment; that when you mince parsley, you use the heads only; that fresh lemon juice is better than bottled lemon juice; and that vegetables vary in size and juiciness. In short, a cook knows that almost all cookery is more-or-less and that you have to make adjustments as you go along; one does this automatically. Cooking is also an individual process, and the same recipe made by two different cooks will taste different, even when they followed the same recipe in every detail.

Finally, I wish to apologize for having expounded on what I imagine are obvious truths to the reader of this book. But one never knows, and besides I like to spark the monotony of the many pages of recipes that follow with a little personal talk.

FOOD PLANNING

Call it menu-making for guests, planning the family's food for a week, or deciding what to cook tonight, I can suggest only one thing: keep it simple and cook only what you know will get eaten. More fights have started at the dinner table; arguing at the table is simply not worth it, says this survivor of an endless number of family meals. And remember that all meals, when they are not nutritionally right in themselves, can be balanced with salads, cereals, cheese and/or milk dishes, and fresh vegetables and fruits.

Family meals, as we know only too well, depend on what there is in the house, the number of people who eat together at one time, the cook's mood, and other sordid details of family life. If you have the willpower to make plans and to stick to them, it is best to make menus for every day of the week. For the main meal (breakfast and lunch can be standard—cereal, toast, juice, sandwiches, soup, et cetera), look at the paper for what is cheap, on sale, or in season, and make a list. Shop once or at most twice a week (even lettuce keeps for days), and once a month, go to one of the supermarket giants in the suburbs and stock up on life's indispensable nonedibles and staples. All this takes a lot of character, and if you don't have it, don't worry but feel at one with the majority of cooks.

But be sure to keep the makings of simple family meals on hand, things like pasta, canned tomato sauce, canned chili, corned beef, and other canned or frozen foods—especially canned or frozen fruit will jolly up a meal. Canned peaches with ice cream—delicious, I say. I also keep frozen meals in the freezer, since the cost for my husband and me is not so great as to matter. While I eat weight-controlled, he eats free-range, and everything is a long way from the TV dinner of yore. (No, I am not thinking of the so-called "gourmet" frozen foods of famous chefs, but of honest supermarket stuff which is reasonably priced.) I advise any cook to have frozen dishes on hand, whether boughten or homemade (preferably divided into portions before freezing). Cooking ahead of time will keep you cool in the summer (you can cook at night or early in the morning and days, weeks, even months in advance) and keep you peaceful when you are rushed at mealtimes. Today many families eat together only on Sundays or for Sunday brunch, what with every member being gainfully or intellectually or sportingly employed outside the home at normal mealtimes. You must be able to put some decent hot food on the table quickly, and if you are not a fast, controlled cook, don't try to get a full meal on the table in fifteen or thirty minutes as some cookbooks will promise naïve readers. Instead, rely on your trusty freezer or can opener, and make the folks eat some raw vegetables and fruit for balance.

But be on time with your meals, whether for a whole family or for one member. Being kept waiting for food is horrible. If it bothers you to be interrupted in your kitchen work by visitors, throw them out ruthlessly, pointing out that they need your food more than you need their company at the given moment. It is also nice not to slop the food all over the dish or plate when serving it. For every day, you don't need to gussy up the food—you don't wear gussied-up clothes every day—but be neat, neat, neat. Better to have your plate resemble Stonehenge than a swamp where everything runs into one another. The single touch of beauty, as exemplified by a sprig of parsley or slice of tomato, makes a plate full of food look better, but it is not essential and entirely between the cook and her sense of what is due to the others—talking of family food, that is. And please, no milk cartons on the table. Also, if you eat in the kitchen, try to straighten up the kitchen before sitting down to your dinner. Looking at cooked-in saucepans is dismal. If you can't wash up as you go along, which is a matter of training oneself (I know this from experience, since I too was a messy cook and am now a tidy one), hide pots, pans, and whatever in the sink or wherever they are out of sight. If you are compulsive about washing up (or getting the kids or spouse to wash up) immediately after dinner, you can get the memories of the meal out of mind at once. If you do things late at night or the next morning, keep them hidden if you think you are going to feel guilty about not washing up.

I think it is a good idea to teach the children to wash up properly and to set the table nicely, though I admit that the task is not accomplished in one session and that it may lead to words. But in later life my sons have told me they were glad to know how to do both properly, and went so far as to say that the one thing they associate with their mother was her shrieking, "Do not stack dishes at the table! It is the most revolting of all revolting habits."

ENTERTAINING

Menu-making should apply to all meals, but in my experience, people—including myself—think of it as something you do when you have guests. Remember above all not to try to impress with the clever-serene-hostess attitude when you are cook, hostess, and waitress at the same time. I mean the chiffon-trailing attitude—it cannot be done, that is all. You have to have good trained servants to be able to ignore the mechanics of having guests. Do what you can do easily without acquiring the face of a tired, patient saint, and do it as well as you can. Nobody will hold disasters against you if you don't fake things in the first place—don't dwell upon them. No explanations, no excuses is my motto; you don't have to impress friends. You'll find out that almost everybody is happy to sit in somebody else's house for a change and to get some food (even if only franks or bread and cheese) they had nothing to do with. But however simple your fare, it should be the best of its kind that you can afford, and cooked and dished up as nicely as you know how— intentions really count in this. If, on the other hand, you have to or want to impress guests, take them to a good restaurant where you know they'll be happy and feel flattered that you want only the best for them. Don't spare the cost; if you want to impress, you have to accept that it is not cheap. I think eight people is the largest number for a sit-down dinner party even when there is enough help. But I warn you that the man-woman, man-woman seating of guests does not work out with eight unless you or your spouse (just one—not both) moves one seat over from the head or foot of the table. But if two of the same sex sit next to each other, the hell with it, I say. Who cares? *I* don't live so formally that this would matter, and fur- thermore, I invite people, not members of a sex. I have found it most practical to seat guests according to a list I carry in my head. I put the food on a sideboard for people to help themselves. If I have a larger number of guest, I make it a buffet with help who serve from behind the table to avoid crushing and messing up the dishes, and to help remove the dirty places and refill the glasses. The few times I had a large cocktail party, I had the affair catered, complete with dishes, glasses, and help.

I have learned that every party needs at least one pretty and one lively woman, and that even in our liberated age it is better to have extra men than extra women, be that as it may. And never, but *never* invite two stars to shine at the same occasion. Even if one is an African explorer and the other performs on the dulcimer, neither star wants to share any glory with another star, no matter how dif- ferent. Also, don't invite bores with amusing people who will know what you are doing and will not be amused to be used as live wires. Invite bores with other bores, and they'll never know the difference.

When it comes to guest food, keep it simple and don't be ostentatious or above yourself. Keep luxury foods such as steaks, roast beef, lobster, etcetera, for the people who honestly cannot afford them but would like a taste. You don't have to compete with a luxury restaurant (you can't anyway—just think of the many chefs, resources such as stocks, sauces, shrimp for garnish only, puff pastry half moons, etcetera, etcetera). People used to fancy cooking welcome honest, very good, and careful home cooking of dishes you rarely find properly made in a restaurant, such as home-fried potatoes, soups, stews, and lovely desserts like Apple Betty and Blueberry Grunt. Become famous for a few specialties, as restaurants do, and you'll reap ample reward for a) simplifying your own life and b) serving dependable meals that c) people will come to eat because you made them. Don't serve too many courses, but serve enough food; do not, however, heap it all at once on a plate. Don't serve controversial or exotic foods unless you know your guests will like them. I found this out when I was left with an uneaten dinner of Turkish specialties for ten guests that I had taken a lot of trouble to make. Chicken, beef, ham, or veal are always safe, whereas lamb and seafood are not necessarily a success. I largely ignore vegetables for dinner parties unless I serve them as a separate course. They tend to be overcooked or almost raw, but I have discovered what every good restaurant knows: puréed vegetables will keep their color, flavor, and will also wait over hot water. But if you have a salad before the main dish, ask yourself if you really need more than a token green or yellow vegetable with the meat. (I don't think that even a token is needed—but then, that is my opinion as a potato lover who does not consider potatoes a vegetable.)

I think it is fun to make a meal out of seasonal foods that usually appear only as side dishes. Asparagus is such a food, and I have served nothing but that (about two pounds, cleaned, for each guest, since it *is* the meal) served with two sauces, accompanied by bread and cheese, and followed by cake. The meal was very successful, as are my chili, beans, guacamole, and *salsa fria* dinners served with champagne. Chili and spicy sauces kill wines, and I don't like beer, but champagne—a good inexpensive bubbly—fits in well with the food and creates a festive atmosphere. Besides, for a crowd (I gave this dinner last year for sixty people), it saves the fuss and bother of drinks and wine service. I have also had a dinner of seven desserts finished with a soup that has been much admired by dessert lovers.

When you don't have a sit-down meal, you must remember that the food must be bite-size or easy to cut with a fork; cutting things up with knife and fork while balancing a plate on your lap is messy. Remember also to have good-size napkins for people eating off their laps, and offer to pay for the cleaning if they spill food that is too unwieldy to eat off one's lap. Don't serve too much food, and don't bother with appetizers for people to whom you will feed dinner. Nobody wants the extra calories. A few nuts are quite enough when you will sit down in a short time to eat a proper dinner. Serve dinner on time and don't let the so-called happy hour drag on for too long; you don't want people to lurch to the table. Serve plenty of wine with your dinner. The wine should be of good quality but not a rare bottle; that is best reserved for true cognoscenti. Enough wine with the food prevents that after-dinner slump in the conversation produced by too many preprandial drinks and late food. Finally, and I can't repeat it too often, don't take things so seriously. It is only a dinner party, and if it is that important to you, take the guests out to eat well with perfect service.

If there is one thing I loathe it is guests who insist on helping when they are not asked to. They mean kindly, I know, but the jumping up and down that ensues is enough to destroy the harmony of any dinner table. I resent guests who don't think me able to manage my own parties (at my age, yet), especially since I feel free and able to ask a friend (before the dinner) to help me if I think it is necessary. The hostess invariably ends up being firm (if not rude) with her guests, telling them to stay put, which is not a nice thing to have to do. To circumvent this unwanted assistance, it is best to have meals with very few courses if you don't have professional help, and to declare as you sit down that you *do not want* any help unless you ask for it, hoping that your guests will mind your words. I can only say I wish they did so more often.

One last word about guests. Try to keep a list of what you serve and to whom and how each food was received. Even if you don't do this systematically, you will accumulate quite a nice bit about meals past that is very useful. And if you can, try to write down the quantities of food you needed. It has helped me to know or to remember that for a curry dinner for 10 I needed 5 pounds of lean, trimmed lamb (I bought about 7 pounds, untrimmed), 3 cups of rice for pilaff, and for a mushroom and watercress salad with lemon juice, 2 pounds of mushrooms, 2 bunches of watercress, and 1½ cups of dressing, plus 1 pound of Stilton, 1 pound of gruyère, and 1 pound of assorted French goat cheese, plus a chocolate cake to end up with.

Hors d'Oeuvres, Appetizers, and Salads

It may seem odd to lump these three categories together, but in fact these dishes frequently overlay—is Russian Mushroom Caviar, for instance, an hors d'oeuvre, an appetizer, or a salad?—and it might be profitable for the home cook to consider their interchangeability.

Europeans do not consider a salad a necessity with every meal the way we do. A salad is served in lieu of other vegetables. Or it may be served as an hors d'oeuvre. This brings us to the question of where the appetizer ends and the hors d'oeuvre begins, or vice versa.

I, for one, have never been able to arrive at a clear-cut solution, but generally speaking, I would say that appetizers are goodies that are eaten standing up, whereas hors d'oeuvres are eaten at the table as the amusing beginning of a meal.

Escoffier and practitioners of the classic French cuisine reserve hors d'oeuvres for luncheon and soup for dinner, though oysters or caviar may take the place of soup.

Thus the choice of how to start a dinner rests squarely with the hostess. She must observe one rule only—that the appetizers or hors d'oeuvres, wherever served, be light and teasing to the palate, and never filling. I also think that these tidbits should not look fussed over by busy little fingers. It is all very well to create a colorful Persian tapestry effect with little morsels of food, but is the food then still really fresh and appetizing? Not to me. Admittedly food must look inviting to the eye before it reaches the palate, but this can easily be done without carrying the quest for sheer beauty too far in a medium not meant for it. Paint if you must, but do not paint with foods, I say.

To come back to salads. Vegetables lend themselves admirably to salads in raw or cooked form. Cauliflower, broccoli, string beans, carrots, and artichokes make excellent salads (and hors d'oeuvres). If they are cooked, the dressing should go on while the vegetables are still hot, so that it can be properly absorbed.

Let us remember that in Europe a fruit salad is a dessert and is not served with lettuce and a French or other dressing. A gelatin dish, too, is a dessert. If a nonsweet substance is jelled, it becomes an aspic and can be admitted to the family of hors d'oeuvres. As for the Europeans' opinions of our habit of serving fruit with mayonnaise, they are better left unexpressed.

SNOW ALMONDS

This comes from a most wonderful Turkish cookbook, The Art of Turkish Cooking *by Neset Eren (Doubleday, 1969), which I treasure above all others. The almonds are as delicious as they are elegant.*

Serves 6 to 10

6 ounces unblanched almonds

Place the almonds into a container with a lid and add cold water to cover the almonds. Cover container and refrigerate for 4 days.

The day before serving, drain the almonds and rub off the skins, which will come off easily. Wash almonds under cold running water and put them back into the container, and again, fill with cold water. Cover and refrigerate. Fill a 6-inch-high glass bowl with water to within 2 inches of the top. Freeze solid.

At serving time, drain almonds and place on top of the ice in the glass bowl. Serve almonds on ice, with predinner drinks.

NOTE: Although the recipe directs you to peel and wash the almonds the day before serving, they can be kept in the refrigerator for about a week before being peeled and washed.

ANGELS ON
HORSEBACK

Two to four oysters or clams serve one.

Bacon
Fresh or canned oysters or clams, shucked and drained
Toast (optional)

Trim the rind from the slices of bacon. Wrap each oyster or clam with 1 slice of bacon. Secure with a toothpick or thread several on a skewer. Broil or bake until bacon is crisp. Serve as is, or remove toothpick or skewer and serve on a round of hot toast.

CHEESE SPREAD

About 1¼ cups

1 cup grated Swiss cheese
¼ cup heavy cream
½ cup butter, at room temperature
3 tablespoons brandy
Salt
Freshly ground pepper
Dash ground nutmeg

Beat together the cheese and cream until the mixture is light. Cream the butter with the brandy. Combine the mixtures and blend thoroughly. Season with salt and pepper to taste, and add the nutmeg. Chill before using. Serve on melba toast.

NOTE: I prefer to do my beating with an electric hand beater, but I think a food processor or KitchenAid can be used, especially for large quantities.

HUNGARIAN CHEESE SPREAD

In Central Europe this fragrant spread, eaten on very dark bread as an accompaniment to beer, is very well known under the name of Liptauer. *This version is not as powerful as real* Liptauer.

About 1½ cups

  1 cup cream cheese or cottage cheese
¾ cup butter
  1 teaspoon paprika
½ teaspoon Dijon mustard
  1 teaspoon caraway seeds
  1 teaspoon chopped chives or minced onion
  2 teaspoons capers, drained
    About 3 tablespoons sour cream
    Salt
    Freshly ground pepper

Cream the cheese and butter. Add the remaining ingredients, and season with salt and pepper to taste. Mix thoroughly. Chill. Serve with crackers, or pumpernickel or French bread, with drinks or as a snack.

ROQUEFORT SPREAD

Simple and tasty for drinks.

About 2½ cups

½ pound Roquefort cheese
1 3-ounce package cream cheese
½ cup sweet butter
¼ cup good quality brandy or Cognac
¼ cup ground walnuts or pecans

Have all the ingredients at room temperature. Beat the Roquefort, cream cheese, and butter together until smooth and perfectly assimilated. Stir in the brandy and stir until mixture is smooth. Add the walnuts and mix well. Turn into a crock and refrigerate for 1 to 3 days to mellow the flavors. Serve with crackers or melba toast.

NOTE: This may also be made in a food processor. Cut the cheeses and butter into small pieces before processing. Process, add the brandy and walnuts, and process again for a few seconds or only until mixture is smooth. Do not overprocess or mixture will liquify.

INSTANT LIVER PÂTÉ SPREAD

About 1 cup

½ pound braunschweiger (smoked liverwurst) or plain liverwurst
½ cup butter, at room temperature
1 tablespoon grated onion
2 tablespoons minced parsley
3 tablespoons good quality brandy or Cognac
Parsley sprigs (optional)

Combine all the ingredients in a bowl, and mash and mix them
thoroughly to obtain a smooth paste. Or blend in a blender or food
processor; in this case you will need an additional 2 to 3 tablespoons
brandy. Shape into a ball and chill. Serve on a plate, surrounded by
parsley sprigs as a garnish if desired.

PÂTÉ FERNANDE

*This country pâté is as easy as meat loaf and doesn't need
special equipment.*

Serves 10

1½ pounds pork liver
1½ pounds lean pork
¾ pound salt pork, blanched
2 eggs
1 teaspoon salt
½ teaspoon freshly ground pepper
⅛ teaspoon dried thyme
1 bay leaf, crumbled fine
2 tablespoons finely chopped onion
1 to 2 tablespoons brandy
½ pound sliced bacon

Preheat the oven to moderate (350° F).

Using a good sharp knife, chop the pork liver, lean pork, and salt
pork as fine as possible, or pass through the finest blade of a meat
grinder. (If the salt pork is very salty, soak first in cold water for 30
minutes or blanch in boiling water to cover for ten minutes. Dry
carefully before using.) Combine meats with the eggs in a bowl.
Work together until eggs are well blended. Add the salt, pepper,
thyme, bay leaf, onion, and brandy, and combine thoroughly. Line a
9-inch loaf pan with bacon strips. Fill with pork mixture. Cover
with the remaining bacon strips. Place loaf pan in a 9 x 13-inch pan.
Pour in enough hot water around loaf pan to come up about ½ inch
from bottom of pan. Bake for 2 hours. Cool before unmolding. Chill
and serve sliced on a bed of lettuce.

Pâté "Supermarket"

A flavorful country-style pâté.

Serves 8 to 10

About 1 pound chicken livers, trimmed, halved, and cut into ¼-inch pieces (about 2 cups)
 1 cup lean pork, cut into ¼-inch pieces (you can use 3 ½-inch-thick center cut pork chops [about 1 to 1½ pounds], bone and fat removed)
 ½ pound pork sausage, thawed if frozen, and crumbled (1 cup packaged)
 ¼ cup port
 ¼ cup dry sherry
 ½ cup brandy
 ¼ cup firmly packed minced parsley
 2 tablespoons finely chopped garlic or shallots
 4½ teaspoons salt
 1 teaspoon dried thyme
 ⅛ teaspoon ground nutmeg
 ⅛ teaspoon ground white pepper
 12 slices bacon, about 7 ounces, each strip cut in half crosswise
 4 bay leaves
 1 envelope (1 tablespoon) unflavored gelatin
 ½ cup dry white wine

In a large bowl, combine the chicken livers, pork pieces, and sausage. Add the port, sherry, brandy, parsley, garlic, salt, thyme, nutmeg, and pepper. Gently mix ingredients until thoroughly combined. Cover and let stand overnight in a cool place or in the refrigerator.

Preheat the oven to high (425° F).

Line the bottom of an 8½ x 4½ x 3-inch loaf pan with 3 slices of the bacon. Line each 8½-inch side with 2 slices bacon and the 4½-inch sides with ½ slice bacon. Carefully spoon the chicken liver mixture into the loaf pan, packing mixture into pan firmly. (Mixture will completely fill pan.) Top with the remaining 4 slices bacon. Garnish top with the bay leaves. Cover pan with aluminum foil.

Place loaf pan in a 13 x 9-inch pan. Pour in enough hot water around loaf pan to come up about ½ inch from bottom of pan. Bake for 1¾ hours, or until completely cooked through. Cool. Carefully pour off pan juices into a small saucepan (about ⅔ cup). In a small bowl, soften the gelatin in the wine. Bring the pan juices to a boil. Add the gelatin mixture. Heat over low heat, stirring until gelatin is dissolved. Pour gelatin mixture over pâté in pan. Chill overnight. To serve, cut into slices.

———

Tuscan Chicken Liver Toasts

I CROSTINI DEL MARCHESE

Tuscans like toast appetizers and make many different kinds, piled with cheese or meat mixtures and different seasonings. Basically, crostini *is the kind of dish you make with what you have on hand, adapting ingredients and cooking times. Serve as an hors d'oeuvre or a first course, as is.*

Serves 6 to 8

¼ cup olive oil
2 tablespoons minced onion
2 tablespoons minced celery
2 tablespoons minced carrot
    About ½ pound chicken meat cut from legs or breast, cut into ¼-inch cubes
    Salt
    Freshly ground pepper
¼ to ⅓ cup dry white wine
½ pound chicken livers, trimmed and chopped
¼ cup capers, drained
4 anchovy fillets, drained
2 tablespoons brandy
⅛ teaspoon ground nutmeg
2 tablespoons butter, at room temperature and cut into small pieces
    About ⅓ cup hot chicken bouillon
1 long loaf French or Italian bread, cut into ½- to ¾-inch slices
    Olive oil

Heat ¼ cup olive oil in a large deep frying pan. Add the onion, celery, and carrot. Cook for about 5 minutes, stirring constantly, until onion is soft and golden but not brown. Add the chicken, season with salt and pepper to taste, and cook for 3 to 4 minutes. Stir in ¼ cup of the wine. Cook over low heat without a cover for about 10 minutes, or until chicken is cooked. Add the chicken livers and mix well. Cook over low heat, stirring frequently, for about 10 minutes. If the mixture looks too dry, add the remaining wine. Add the capers and anchovy fillets, and cook for 5 minutes longer. Stir in the brandy and nutmeg, and cook for 2 to 3 more minutes. Stir in the butter. The mixture should be very thick. Meanwhile, preheat the oven to hot (400° F). Spoon half the mixture into a blender with 2 or 3 tablespoons of the bouillon and purée. Repeat with the remaining mixture. Return all the purée to the frying pan. Over low heat and stirring constantly, cook for about 2 minutes to dry out. Remove from heat and keep warm.

Lay the bread slices on a baking sheet. Brush each with about 1 teaspoon olive oil. Bake for 5 to 10 minutes, or until toasted golden brown. Spread each slice with some of the chicken liver mixture and serve immediately, very hot.

MADRAS ANCHOVY TOAST

This recipe goes back to 1860 and is ideal for a chafing dish.

Serves 2 to 4

- 2 tablespoons butter
- 2 egg yolks
- 1 tablespoon dry sherry or beer
- 2 teaspoons anchovy paste or sauce
  Cayenne pepper
  Hot toast fingers

Melt the butter in a double boiler or chafing dish. Add the egg yolks and beat well with a fork. Add the sherry, anchovy paste, and cayenne pepper to taste, and mix thoroughly. Spread on hot toast fingers or serve hot as a dip.

RUSSIAN MUSHROOM CAVIAR

Serves 2 to 4

2 tablespoons olive oil
1 medium onion, minced
½ pound mushrooms, finely chopped
 Salt
 Freshly ground pepper
1 tablespoon fresh lemon juice
2 tablespoons minced chives
1 tablespoon sour cream (optional)
 Tomato slices

Heat the olive oil and cook the onion until soft. Add the mushrooms and cook until just soft. Add salt and pepper to taste and the lemon juice. Add chopped chives, and the sour cream if desired. Chill before serving garnished with tomato slices.

CAPONATA ALLA SICILIANA

There is no English word for this pickled vegetable concoction—it is sold in cans or jars under the name caponatina *or its diminutive. Since it is one of the best, it is worth making at home and storing in either sterilized jars or in the refrigerator.*

About 2 quarts

     4 medium eggplants
   1½ cups olive oil
     4 large onions, sliced
     1 cup Italian canned tomatoes, forced through a sieve
     4 stalks celery, diced small
     ½ cup capers, drained
     ½ cup chopped parsley
    12 black olives, pitted and coarsely chopped
     1 tablespoon pine nuts (optional)
     ½ cup wine vinegar
     ¼ cup sugar
     ½ teaspoon salt
     ½ teaspoon freshly ground pepper

Peel and dice the eggplants. Heat 1 cup of the olive oil and fry the eggplant until soft and brown. Remove eggplant, add the remaining ½ cup oil, and cook the onions. Add the tomatoes and celery, and cook until celery is tender. To prevent scorching, add a little water if necessary. Add the capers, parsley, olives, pine nuts if used, and fried eggplant. Heat the vinegar in a small saucepan. Dissolve the sugar in the vinegar and pour over eggplant mixture. Add the salt and pepper, and simmer without a cover gently over very low heat for about 20 minutes, stirring frequently. Cool before serving.

FRENCH EGGS IN ASPIC

OEUFS EN GELÉE

The following recipe is the classic one, as it appears in thousands of French restaurants and homes almost daily. Oeufs en gelée *also make a good luncheon or buffet dish.*

Serves 6 as an appetizer, 3 as a main dish

---

  6 eggs
1½ cups clear chicken consommé
  1 envelope (1 tablespoon) unflavored gelatin soaked in ¼ cup cold water
  2 tablespoons Madeira or port
  6 thin slices cooked ham
    Fresh tarragon leaves or tiny parsley sprigs
    Tomato slices
    Capers

Boil the eggs for 6 minutes and cool under cold running water. Shell eggs very carefully since they are still soft. Reserve. Heat the chicken consommé, add the gelatin soaked in water, and stir until gelatin is completely dissolved. Add the Madeira. Cool aspic but do not jell.

Use small molds, ramekins, cups, or bowls that are just large enough to hold 1 egg each and 1 slice of ham. Trim ham to fit the top of the molds. Pour a ¼-inch-deep layer of aspic into each mold. Chill aspic until almost but not quite firm. Place 2 crossed leaves of tarragon or a tiny sprig of parsley on aspic. Gently place an egg in each mold. Spoon aspic over eggs until mold is almost filled. Cover each egg with a trimmed piece of ham. Spoon a little more aspic over ham. Chill eggs until aspic is set. Dip molds for *just an instant* in hot water and unmold on a bed of lettuce. Decorate with slices of tomato topped with a few capers.

French Anchovy Eggs with Garlic

OEUFS AUX ANCHOIS ET À L'AIL

A sight familiar to the patron of inexpensive French restaurants is half a hard-boiled egg decorated with crisscrossed anchovy fillets and reposing on a leaf of lettuce.

Here is a more interesting way of making this simple hors d'oeuvre, which combines anchovies and garlic, both so beloved by the French of Provence.

Serves 4 to 6

2 cloves garlic
4 anchovy fillets, drained
8 capers
3 tablespoons olive oil
1 teaspoon wine vinegar
  Salt
  Freshly ground pepper
6 hard-boiled eggs
  Lettuce leaves
  Parsley

Chop and crush the garlic. Add the anchovy fillets and capers, and mash with a fork into a smooth paste. Blend in the olive oil and vinegar, and add salt and pepper to taste. Shell the hard-boiled eggs and cut into quarters. Cover with the sauce. Serve on lettuce leaves and decorate with parsley.

RUSSIAN HORS D'OEUVRE CASSEROLE

DRAGOMIROVSKY VORSCHMACK

———

To the unknown Dragomirov, this may have been but a favorite hors d'oeuvre (vorschmack means "a before-taste"). To me, it is also a very adequate way of using leftovers for a rather nice luncheon or supper main dish.

———

Serves 4 to 6

———

2 tablespoons butter
¼ cup minced onion
½ to 1 cup chopped mushrooms
1 cup any diced leftover cooked meat
1 cup diced cooked ham
1 cup diced cooked chicken
1 cup diced boiled potatoes
1 dill pickle, diced
½ cup olives (either green or black), pitted and diced
   Salt
   Freshly ground pepper
1 to 1½ cups sour cream
2 hard-boiled eggs, chopped
2 to 3 tomatoes, sliced
½ cup grated Parmesan, cheddar, or Swiss cheese

Preheat the oven to moderate (350° F).

Heat the butter and cook the onion. Add the mushrooms and cook until just tender. Combine with the meat, ham, chicken, potatoes, pickle, and olives. Add salt and pepper to taste. Mix with the sour cream. Turn mixture into a 2½- to 3-quart buttered baking dish and cover with the hard-boiled eggs. Surround with tomato slices. Sprinkle grated cheese over the top and bake until thoroughly heated and brown.

———

BELGIAN ENDIVE, WALNUT, AND SWISS CHEESE SALAD

An excellent first course as well as a good buffet salad, since it won't wilt. Ingredients can be halved, doubled, or tripled at will. The cheese must be Swiss, preferably imported from Switzerland, though domestic Swiss will do.

Serves 6

    6 medium to large Belgian endives
 1½ cups shelled walnuts, broken into ½-inch pieces
 1½ cups shredded (not grated) Swiss cheese
  ¼ cup minced parsley or chives (optional)
    1 cup vinaigrette (preferably made with white wine vinegar)

Wash and dry the Belgian endives, and trim. Cut Belgian endives into 1-inch rounds and place in a salad bowl. Scatter the walnuts over Belgian endives, and scatter the cheese over Belgian endives and walnuts. Sprinkle with the parsley or chives. Pour the vinaigrette over salad and toss at the table.

NOTE: When making the vinaigrette, remember that the cheese may be salty. Consult your favorite standard cookbook for a vinaigrette recipe.

Belgian endives are tight, white 3- to 4-inch cylinder-shaped vegetables and completely different from the lettuce-type green endive. Since people have been known to confuse the two, it is wise to refer to the Belgian endive by its proper name.

CELERY ROOT AND POTATO SALAD

This salad used to be one of the many specialties of the Hotel Adlon in Berlin, one of the great European hotels in the days of the Kaiser.

Serves 4 to 6

3 large or 5 small celery roots
¾ cup white vinegar
3 large or 5 small potatoes
3 red apples
⅔ to ¾ cup mayonnaise thinned with fresh lemon juice to the consistency of thin pancake batter
Salt
Freshly ground pepper
Watercress
Black truffles or black olives

Cook the celery roots in salted water to cover for about 15 to 25 minutes, or until just tender. Peel while hot. Remove woody core, if any, and cut into 1-inch julienne strips. Marinate immediately in half the vinegar, or celery root will darken. Cook potatoes at the same time as the celery root, but separately. Peel potatoes while still hot, cut into 1-inch julienne strips, and marinate in remaining vinegar while hot. (If marinated cold, the vegetables will not be so tasty.) Keep celery root and potatoes in separate marinades for about 30 minutes. Combine vegetables, but do not drain. Quarter and core apples, but do not peel. Cut into 1-inch julienne strips and add immediately to vegetables, or apples will darken. Drain surplus vinegar from salad, taking care not to break the julienne strips. Add the mayonnaise, season with salt and pepper to taste, and blend thoroughly. Line a salad bowl (in Germany glass bowls are used) with a bed of washed watercress that has been shaken dry. Pile salad in the middle to form a dome. Smooth down and garnish with slices of truffles or black olives.

MIXED SALAD NIÇOISE WITH RAVIGOTE SAUCE

SALADE NIÇOISE RAVIGOTE

This is one of the versions of salade niçoise, *a French equivalent of our chef's salad but spicier. It is a perfect main dish for a luncheon or a hot summer day. The olives in it must be black, never green.*

Serves 4 to 6

CUT INTO THIN JULIENNE STRIPS:
1 cup cooked cold chicken
2 slices lean ham
4 to 6 slices Italian salami
 Whites of 3 hard-boiled eggs
1 can anchovy fillets, drained
1 medium boiled beet

DICE:
2 medium cold boiled potatoes
1 unpeeled small tart apple
2 stalks celery
1 sweet pepper, green or red

 1 head crisp lettuce, shredded
 About 15 black olives (Italian or Greek are best)
 Ravigote Sauce (*see below*)
 Lemon slices and black olives

Rub a wooden salad bowl with a cut clove of garlic. (This is not a garlicky salad, though garlic may be added to taste.) Toss together all the ingredients and pile up in a mound. Chill until serving time. Then pour about ¾ cup Ravigote Sauce over the salad. Garnish with thin slices of lemon and more black olives.

 MY OWN RAVIGOTE SAUCE
8 fresh tarragon sprigs or 1½ teaspoons dried tarragon
⅓ cup watercress leaves (stems must be removed)

 1 tablespoon chopped chives
 1 small clove garlic, minced
 1 tablespoon chopped parsley
 ½ teaspoon prepared mustard (preferably Dijon)
 2 tablespoons white vinegar (preferably wine vinegar)
 ¾ cups olive oil
    Salt
    Freshly ground pepper

With the back of a heavy knife on a cutting board, pound together
the tarragon, watercress, chives, garlic, and parsley to make a paste.
In a small bowl, blend the mustard, vinegar, and olive oil. Add herb
paste and stir until smooth. Season with salt and pepper to taste.
Stir again before using.

Orange, Belgian Endive, and Cheese Salad

A good first course, or use as a luncheon or supper salad.

Serves 6

Dressing
¾ cup olive oil
¼ cup white wine vinegar or white vinegar
2 teaspoons Dijon mustard
1 teaspoon salt
¼ cup fresh orange juice

4 large navel oranges
6 medium Belgian endives
½ pound Swiss cheese, cut into ½-inch cubes

Combine all the ingredients for the dressing in a jar. Close the jar tightly and shake to blend. Refrigerate dressing, covered, until serving time.

Peel the oranges and remove every bit of white membrane. Cut into sections, and remove seeds and membrane between sections. Turn into a bowl, cover, and chill until serving time. Cut and trim the Belgian endives, wrap in paper towels, and chill until serving time. Turn the cheese into a bowl, cover, and refrigerate until serving time (the ingredients should be chilled but not frozen).

At serving time, cut the Belgian endives into rounds and turn into a salad bowl. Add the cheese and orange sections. Shake the dressing before adding it to the salad bowl. Toss at the table.

TOMATOES STUFFED WITH SHRIMP

TOMATES AUX CREVETTES

This is Belgium's favorite first course, made with that country's tiny shrimp. You may use chopped shrimp, of course, but I prefer the tiny imported Danish shrimp or the tiny Pacific shrimp, both available canned or frozen.

Serves 4

---

4 large, firm, ripe tomatoes
1⅓ to 1½ cups cooked shrimp, chopped, or tiny canned shrimp, drained
About 1 cup well-seasoned lemon mayonnaise
Salt
Freshly ground pepper
Dash cayenne pepper
2 tablespoons minced parsley, chervil, fresh dillweed, or chives
Lettuce leaves

Cut a slice from the top of each tomato and reserve. Carefully hollow out the tomatoes with a teaspoon, taking care not to break the shell. (Save pulp for sauce.) Invert the tomatoes on a plate and let drain for 20 minutes. Combine the shrimp and about ¾ cup of the mayonnaise. Season with salt, pepper, and cayenne pepper to taste. Fill the tomatoes with the shrimp mixture. Spoon some of the remaining mayonnaise over each shrimp-filled tomato, smooth it, and sprinkle with some of the parsley or other herbs. Replace the reserved top slices on the filled tomatoes, but at a slight angle so that the mayonnaise and parsley show. Line a platter or individual plates with lettuce leaves and top with the tomatoes. Refrigerate until serving time.

Soups

Few foods have had more nonsense written about them than soups. In America today, the high priests of the ladle either go into raptures over voluptuous cream soups, in which much cream is made even more hedonistic by the addition of soupçons of this or that stylish ingredient. Or they have a touching faith, worthy of a better cult, in the character- and body-building qualities of "real peasant soups."

Leaving the hedonists to drown in their floods of cream, let us remember that soup is the mainstay of so many peasants because it is the most inexpensive and filling food for people who can't afford meat every day. In soup, every bit of vegetable and scrap of meat goes a long way; it saves fuel where fuel is expensive since it takes but little to cook a lot.

As for the assumption that admirable character traits are in some way associated with peasant soups, it might be pointed out that backwardness, cupidity, and narrowmindedness are also traits typically found in peasants. If there *is* any connection between soup and character, perhaps it is best not to draw parallels too closely. If we do, the abominations found in some fashionable soups might reflect unfavorably on both their originators and their admirers.

Formerly, in Europe at least, soup almost invariably started the dinner. It is a pity this is no longer the case, since a well-chosen soup does pleasant service in warming the stomach before the arrival of more solid food. But the point is to warm it, not to surfeit it.

Soup preceding a substantial dinner should be neither too rich nor served in too large a quantity. A cup of good strong bouillon meets these requirements admirably, especially if served with perhaps a dash of sherry and a simple little garnish—a sprinkling of cheese, a few sprigs of watercress, or a slice of cooked carrot or string bean. How well the genuine *haute cuisine* thinks of this treatment can be seen by turning to the *Concise Encyclopaedia of Gastronomy* by the late André Simon, one of the world's greatest authorities on food and wine. Simon lists forty-three ways of garnishing consommé. Escoffier, in his cookbook, lists eighty-four!

The mystique so often associated with soup runs rampant in many people when they come to the making of soup stock or bouillon. In this the Italians are leaders, since they firmly believe in what can only be called the graillike qualities of *il brodo* (bouillon) as the healer of all bodily and mental distress. In times past there were few Italian homes that were not constantly permeated by the smell of simmering soup meat—not a strong but a most insinuating smell, very much like that of wet blotting paper. Canned bouillons and bouillon cubes are now clearing up the atmosphere. This is all to the good, I think, especially since the European (notably Swiss) brands are really excellent—noticeably better than the American varieties.

But here in America we still have purists who scorn methods less laborious than those employed by the great chefs of old-time France. We also have the faddists who advocate that all tired food parings and scraps, all miserable bits of bone and gristle—*everything*—must go into the pot for soup stock. And their soup pots become self-perpetuating horrors, always simmering away on the back of the stove—forever with us, like taxes.

For the purists among my readers I give the basic bouillon recipes to make from scratch for soups and sauces. However, I must warn these enterprising souls that making basic stocks is neither a quick nor inexpensive process, because if they are to taste and look right, they must be made in the classic, slow way and with the correct ingredients. And the clarifying of bouillon, to make it into clear consommé, is scarcely a diverting operation.

Far be it for me to dampen these readers' cooking enthusiasm. . . . Yet I must state my own opinion that today's canned clear broths are about as good as, if not better than, most made at home. I refer to the better brands available in specialty stores, and I suggest using them without dilution for the final success of a dish.

For the reader still determined to make consommé in the grand manner, I can only recommend that he be guided by the old Duke of Bedford. His grandson, in his delightful autobiography *A Silver-plated Spoon* (1959), tells how this noble old party invariably had, for his first course, one cup of beef consommé. But what consommé! Precisely nine and a half pounds of the best shin of beef were required to make one cup. It was made exactly the same way every day, and only one special kitchen maid was entrusted with the making of it. Even after she married, this kitchen maid was induced to return to the house just to perform this single duty.

When serving soup, please remember that cold or iced soups should be thin in consistency, hot ones thicker. Do not oversalt, since almost all soup ingredients are naturally salty. Serve soups hot but not boiling hot, so they can be eaten immediately after serving and don't need to cool down; cooled-down soups get cold too quickly. I do not presume to tell how much soup to serve or to eat. A standard soup serving is one cup, but this can be too little, depending on the soup, the meal that follows, and the soup-eater's desires.

Crackers or bread with soup? That depends on you, the soup-eater, and on the circumstances, as above.

A FEW EXPLANATORY NOTES ON SOUP MAKING

Consommé is clear broth, or bouillon that has been clarified. In the following recipes, they can be interchanged.

The bones for bouillon should be in small pieces and cracked. I feel the meat of the cooked bouillon is not worth eating, though it can be used chopped or sliced for those who feel differently.

It is possible to make all of the following soups with either beef, chicken, or veal bouillon or consommé, or with vegetable bouillon if a meatless soup is desired. Naturally, the flavor of the soup will vary, depending on the liquid used. The kind of bouillon specified in the recipes is what makes the soup authentic.

SKIMMING. Meticulous skimming is essential in all soup making (and in other slow cooking), since it affects the flavor and the aspect of the bouillon, especially if it is to be clarified later for consommé. Skimming is done with a slotted spoon. When the impurities rise to the surface as the soup is boiling, producing scum, they are lifted off with the spoon. During the skimming, a tablespoonful of cold water is added to the soup from time to time, since it brings more scum to the surface to be lifted off. Skimming also includes wiping the inside of the soup pot with a damp, clean cloth down to the high-water mark, since the clearness of the soup depends on the total removal of scum. Broadly speaking, a soup should be skimmed at least three or four times before being allowed to boil or simmer.

DEGREASING BOUILLON. To remove a good deal of the grease, strain the bouillon through a triple layer of cheesecloth or a piece of flannel that has been wet and wrung out. More can be removed by blotting the surface of the bouillon with unglazed brown paper or paper towels. However, the simplest way is to chill the bouillon in the coldest part, or in the freezing compartment, of the refrigerator. The grease then rises to the top and can be lifted off easily in one slab after loosening the edges from the container with a knife. Remaining particles are removed with a slotted spoon.

TO CLARIFY BOUILLON FOR CONSOMMÉ. Clarified bouillon becomes consommé. The *haute cuisine* knows various ways of doing this, but the simplified method that follows is sufficient for the purposes of the recipes in this book.

The bouillon should be cold and clear, since a muddy bouillon will not clarify well. It is better not to use a pan made of aluminum; aluminum tends to cloud the bouillon further. For each quart of bouillon, use the white and shell of 1 egg. Beat the white lightly, then add the crushed shell and 2 teaspoons cold water. Add this mixture to the cold bouillon. Bring to a boil over moderate heat and let boil for 3 minutes, stirring constantly. Remove from heat and let stand undisturbed for 20 to 30 minutes. Strain through a fine sieve lined with a triple layer of cheesecloth. Cool, and store in the refrigerator.

BEEF BOUILLON

For soups, sauces, and other dishes.

About 2 quarts (8 cups)

1 veal knuckle, cracked
1 pound beef brisket or shin
1 beef knuckle, cracked
2 leeks, white and green parts, sliced (when in season)
1 large onion stuck with 2 whole cloves
2 stalks celery with tops, sliced
1 carrot, sliced
3 sprigs parsley
3 quarts cold water
2 teaspoons salt

Place all the ingredients except the salt in a soup kettle. Cover and slowly bring to a boil. Skim as needed. Simmer, covered, over very low heat for 2 hours. Add the salt and simmer for 3 more hours. Strain bouillon through a fine sieve lined with a triple layer of cheesecloth. Chill; remove fat. Store covered in refrigerator, where it will keep for 4 to 5 days, or freeze.

WHITE VEAL STOCK OR BOUILLON

Use in sauce recipes that call for veal bouillon and in other dishes. Since it is delicate in flavor, it can be used in place of chicken bouillon. I think veal bouillon is worth making because, as far as I know, it cannot be bought canned.

About 2 quarts (8 cups)

5 pounds veal bones, including knuckle, cracked
1 pound veal, cut into pieces
2 pounds chicken backs and wings
3 quarts cold water
2 stalks celery with tops, sliced
1 medium to large onion
1 carrot, sliced
3 sprigs parsley
2 teaspoons salt

Cover the veal bones, veal, and chicken parts with water, and boil until the scum rises. Skim and drain. Place bones, veal, and chicken parts in a soup kettle with 3 quarts water and the remaining ingredients. Bring to a boil and simmer, covered, over very low heat for 5 hours, skimming as needed. Strain bouillon through a fine sieve lined with a triple layer of cheesecloth. Chill; remove fat. Store covered in refrigerator, where it will keep for 4 to 5 days, or freeze.

CHICKEN BOUILLON

About 2 quarts (8 cups)

1 3- to 5-pound stewing chicken
1 veal knuckle, cracked
2 pounds chicken backs and wings
3 quarts cold water
1 onion stuck with 2 whole cloves
1 stalk celery with top, sliced
1 carrot, sliced
1 bay leaf
2 teaspoons salt

Place all the ingredients in a soup kettle. Cover and slowly bring to a boil. Skim as needed. Simmer, covered, over low heat, for 3 hours. Strain bouillon through a fine sieve lined with a triple layer of cheesecloth. Chill; remove fat. Store covered in refrigerator, where it will keep for 4 to 5 days, or freeze.

NOTE: Remove fowl from bouillon when the breast is tender. Cut the entire breast off the carcass and return the carcass to the kettle and continue simmering. The breast can be used in any dish that calls for cooked chicken.

VEGETABLE BROTH

Sometimes a vegetable broth is needed for soups or for cooking vegetables or making gravies.

About 1½ quarts (6 cups)

1 large onion, sliced
2 carrots, sliced
2 stalks celery with tops, chopped
8 sprigs parsley
2 to 3 leeks, white and green parts, sliced
2 large fresh tomatoes, chopped
2 quarts cold water
1 tablespoon salt

Place all the ingredients in a soup kettle. Combine vegetables with water and salt. Simmer, covered, over very low heat for 1½ hours. Strain bouillon through a fine sieve lined with a triple layer of cheesecloth. Clarify, if needed, with 1 egg white and the crushed shell of 1 egg. Store covered in the refrigerator, where it will keep for 3 days, or freeze.

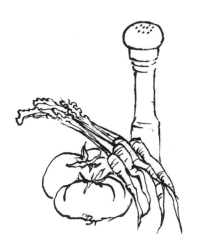

SPANISH SAFFRON BOUILLON

This bouillon should be served in cups, with a sprig of watercress in each serving. The saffron gives the bouillon a charming flavor as well as color. I had it in Cádiz, the whitest of all white Spanish cities.

About 1¾ quarts (7 cups)

1 teaspoon finely grated onion
6 cups hot strong chicken or beef bouillon
  Salt
  Freshly ground white pepper
¾ teaspoon saffron, powdered or threads

Blend the grated onion with ½ cup of the bouillon and add salt and pepper to taste. Dissolve the saffron in another ½ cup of the bouillon. Stir both mixtures into the remaining bouillon and heat through.

NOTE: For a neater soup or other dish cooked with saffron threads rather than powdered saffron, strain out the threads (after they have served their flavoring and coloring purpose) before adding the saffron to the other ingredients. I never do, but you might be that much more particular.

SWISS MUSHROOM BOUILLON

CONSOMMÉ AUX CHAMPIGNONS

———

This soup, a light and invigorating curtain raiser for a meal, is typical of the fine cooking in Swiss hotels. Serve it in cups rather than plates and accompanied by Cheese Balls (see page 79).

———

About 1¾ quarts (7 cups)

———

½ pound mushrooms, finely chopped
6 cups hot strong beef bouillon
  Salt
  Freshly ground pepper
1 cup good dry sherry, warmed but not boiled

Simmer the mushrooms in the bouillon in a covered pan until tender. Add salt and pepper to taste. Heat through. Just before serving, stir in the sherry.

———

CLEAR BORSCH

A quick version of the original recipe.

About 1¾ quarts (7 cups)

2 to 2½ cups canned, drained beets, sliced or coarsely chopped
   Beet juice and water to make 3 cups
3 cups hot beef bouillon
   Salt
   Freshly ground pepper
½ fresh or pickled cucumber, thinly sliced
   Fresh dill, minced
   Sour cream

Cover the beets with the beet juice and water, and simmer covered for 45 minutes, or until beets are pale. Drain, save stock, and discard beets. Add the bouillon to stock. Cover and simmer for about 10 minutes. Add salt and pepper to taste. Serve hot, or chilled in cups. Garnish each serving with cucumber slices and a sprinkling of dill. Pass sour cream separately.

UKRAINIAN BORSCH

About 2½ quarts (10 cups)

1 pound beef chuck, cut into slices
8 cups beef bouillon
   Salt
   Freshly ground pepper
1 bay leaf
2 tablespoons butter
1 large onion, chopped
2 carrots, sliced
3 medium beets, shredded
½ medium cabbage, shredded
1 tablespoon minced parsley
1 8-ounce can tomato sauce
1 tablespoon vinegar
2 medium potatoes, cubed
2 to 3 tablespoons grated peeled raw beets
   Fresh dill, minced
   Sour cream

Put the beef into a soup kettle with the bouillon. Add salt and pepper to taste, and the bayleaf. Bring to a boil, skim, and simmer, covered, for about 30 minutes.

In another pan, heat the butter and cook the onion, carrots, beets, cabbage, and parsley for 3 to 4 minutes. Add the tomato sauce and vinegar, and simmer over low heat for about 10 minutes. Add vegetable mixture to beef and bouillon, add the potatoes, and simmer, covered, for about 1 hour; or until meat is tender. Skim when needed. Season with salt and pepper to taste. Add the grated raw beets to the soup for the last 10 minutes of cooking. Remove beef to a separate platter, slice, and serve separately. Serve soup in bowls with a sprinkling of dill over each serving. Pass sour cream separately.

MADAME GORIS'S BELGIAN LAMB SOUP

About 2½ quarts (10 cups)

1½ pounds lamb breast riblets, excess fat removed
2 quarts water
   Salt
1 14- to 16-ounce can plum or whole tomatoes (see Note)
3 inner stalks celery with some leaves, thinly sliced and leaves chopped
1 carrot, diced
1 medium onion, diced
1 medium potato, diced
   Freshly ground pepper
¼ cup Madeira (optional)
   Minced parsley

In a large kettle, cover the lamb riblets with the water. Add 1 table-spoon salt. Drain liquid from the tomatoes and add liquid to kettle. Cut up tomatoes and reserve. Bring riblet mixture to a boil. Reduce the heat and simmer, covered, for 3 hours. Chill thoroughly, or until fat from lamb has solidified. Remove solidified fat from lamb broth and discard. Remove meat, bones, and cartilage from riblets. Cut meat into small pieces and return to broth. Discard bones and carti-lage. Stir in the celery, carrot, onion, potato, and the reserved toma-toes. Cover and simmer for about 1 hour, or until vegetables are tender. Taste and season with salt, if necessary, and some pepper. If desired, add Madeira. Garnish each serving with parsley before serving.

NOTE: You may use 8 ripe medium tomatoes, chopped, instead of canned tomatoes; add when other vegetables are added. Or omit canned tomatoes, increase water to 2½ quarts, and add 1 6-ounce can tomato paste when vegetables are added.

NORWEGIAN SPINACH SOUP

About 1¾ quarts (7 cups)

2 pounds fresh spinach, chopped, or 2 10-ounce packages frozen
  chopped spinach
6 cups hot beef bouillon
3 tablespoons butter
2 tablespoons flour
  Salt
  Freshly ground pepper
2 teaspoons sugar

Cook the spinach in the bouillon for 5 to 10 minutes, or until just tender. Drain, reserving liquid. Keep spinach hot. Melt the butter and stir in the flour, avoiding lumps. Blend into spinach liquid and bring to a boil. Add the reserved spinach, salt and pepper to taste, and the sugar. Simmer for about 5 minutes. Serve with thin slices of buttered rye bread.

FRENCH ONION SOUP

SOUPE À L'OIGNON

Another version of the classic French soup, made with white wine or champagne. Ali Bab, greatest of all modern French gastronomes, recommends it as invigorating after a hunt.

About 2½ quarts (8 to 10 cups)

½ cup butter
2 tablespoons salad oil
1 to 2 pounds onions, thickly or thinly sliced, depending on whether a thicker or thinner soup is desired
1 to 2 tablespoons flour
6 cups hot beef bouillon
2 cups dry white wine or champagne
  Salt
  Freshly ground pepper
  French bread, slightly stale and sliced
1 cup freshly graded Parmesan cheese

Heat the butter and oil in a 4-quart casserole. Add the onions and cook over medium heat until soft and dark brown, stirring frequently. Do not allow to burn. Sprinkle the flour over onions and stir until smooth. Add the bouillon and wine, and season with salt and pepper to taste. Simmer, covered, over very low heat for about 1 hour. Place slices of French bread in a tureen or in individual bowls. Pour soup over them; the slices will rise to the surface. Sprinkle the bread with the cheese. Heat in a hot (425° F) oven until cheese is melted.

SWEET PEPPER SOUP

LA SOUPE AUX POIVRONS

About 2 quarts (8 cups)

3 large sweet peppers, green, yellow, or red, or a combination
7 cups well-seasoned chicken or beef bouillon
1 tablespoon tomato paste
¼ teaspoon saffron, powdered or threads
1 teaspoon paprika
  Salt
  Freshly ground pepper
⅛ teaspoon cayenne pepper, or to taste
⅓ cup rice
½ tablespoon minced parsley, chives, or chervil

Wash and dry the peppers. Place them around a burner on the stove. Turn the heat to high. Toast until outer skin is charred; turn frequently with a fork to insure even charring. Using fingers and a sharp paring knife, peel the charred skins off the peppers; to avoid scorching fingers, do this under running water. Cut the peppers in half and remove core, seeds, and membranes. Dry on paper towels and cut into ½-inch squares.

Bring the bouillon to a boil. Add the peppers, tomato paste, saffron, and paprika. Taste for saltiness; if necessary, add salt. Add pepper and cayenne to taste. Sprinkle the rice into the soup. Reduce the heat to medium-low. Cook, covered, until rice is tender. Turn into a soup tureen and serve sprinkled with the parsley, chives or chervil, this latter being the most French herb but hard to get in America unless you grow it yourself or buy it dried.

SWISS LEEK AND RICE SOUP

About 1½ quarts (6 cups)

6 cups beef bouillon (can be made from cubes)
⅓ cup white or brown rice
4 to 5 medium leeks, white and green parts, thinly sliced
1½ cups grated Swiss cheese
14 cups dry white wine
Salt
Freshly ground pepper

Bring the bouillon to a boil. Add the rice and cook over low heat for about 10 minutes, or until the rice is almost tender; brown rice takes longer. Add the leeks and simmer, covered, for 5 to 10 minutes, or until vegetables and rice are tender. In a small saucepan, combine the cheese and wine. Cook over low heat, stirring constantly, until the cheese is melted. Turn the cheese mixture into the leek-rice mixture and blend well. Check the seasoning; if necessary, add salt and pepper to taste. Serve very hot with brown bread and butter.

TURKEY SOUP

The swan song of your Christmas bird, much improved by wine.

About 2¼ quarts (9 to 10 cups)

6 cups water
2 cups dry white wine
1 turkey carcass, cut into pieces
1 cup chopped celery
1 cup chopped carrot
½ cup chopped onion
½ cup canned tomatoes
¼ cup chopped parsley
  Salt
  Freshly ground pepper
4 to 6 tablespoons medium barley or rice

Combine the water, wine, turkey carcass, celery, carrot, onion, tomatoes, and parsley in a large kettle. Season with salt and pepper to taste. Bring to a boil and simmer, covered, for 30 minutes. Strain through a sieve, pressing down on the vegetables to extract all their juice. Bring again to a boil. Sprinkle in the barley and simmer until tender. Add more barley or rice if you want a thicker soup. Or if you want a thinner one, add a little more wine or water.

TURKISH YOGURT SOUP

A thin, pale, and rather tart soup that does well with a dinner featuring roast meat. The soup must be kept thin and served very hot.

About 1⅔ quarts (7 cups)

2 cups plain yogurt
6 cups hot beef bouillon
1 tablespoon butter
1 tablespoon flour
2 tablespoons chopped fresh or dried mint

Stir or whisk the yogurt into the bouillon. Keep hot, but do not let boil or soup will curdle. In another saucepan, melt the butter and stir in the flour, blending thoroughly, and cook for 3 to 4 minutes. Do not allow to brown. Carefully pour the yogurt-bouillon mixture into the blended flour and butter, stirring constantly. Bring to one quick boil—no more—stirring constantly. Just before serving, sprinkle with the mint.

TUSCAN MUSHROOM AND TOMATO SOUP

ACQUA COTTA

The literal translation of acqua cotta *is "cooked water," but this tasty soup is anything but that.*

About 2½ quarts (10 cups)

¼ cup olive oil
2 cloves garlic
1 pound mushrooms, cut into thin slices
1 pound fresh tomatoes, peeled and chopped, or 2 to 3 cups drained canned plum tomatoes, chopped
Salt
Freshly ground pepper
½ teaspoon dried marjoram
5 to 6 cups hot water
2 eggs
½ cup freshly grated Parmesan cheese
6 slices Italian bread, toasted

Heat the olive oil in a large saucepan. Cook the garlic until browned, then discard. Add the mushrooms to the oil and cook over medium heat, stirring constantly, for about 5 minutes. Add the tomatoes and mix well. Season with salt and pepper to taste, and add the marjoram and the water. Simmer, covered, over low heat for about 15 minutes. In a soup tureen, beat the eggs with the cheese. Pour the soup over the mixture, stirring to combine soup and eggs. Place the bread on top and serve hot.

NOTE: This soup can be made in half the time given above, but the taste is better when it is simmered longer, since the flavors of the ingredients will have the time to blend properly.

GARDEN VEGETABLE SOUP

This is the best soup of its kind, out of Tuscany. It is a thick soup, akin to a stew, and the reason for its being so incredibly flavorful is that NO water is added to the soup—the vegetables make their own liquid. You must add the vegetables in the order given for the right results. It is best when made with fava beans. I consider this my most successful soup, the year round.

About 3 quarts (12 cups)

2 large tomatoes, peeled and sliced, or 2 cups canned tomatoes, drained and chopped
2 medium onions, thinly sliced
1 large clove garlic, minced, or to taste
2 large zucchini, sliced
1 medium head romaine lettuce, shredded
2 pounds fresh peas, shelled, or 1 10-ounce package frozen peas
1 cup minced parsley sprigs
2 tablespoons minced fresh basil leaves or 1 teaspoon dried basil
2 pounds fresh fava beans, shelled, or 1 10-ounce package frozen lima beans
⅓ to ½ cup good olive oil
   Salt
   Freshly ground pepper
   Freshly grated Parmesan cheese

Spread the tomatoes over the bottom of a deep 3-quart casserole that can go to the table. Top the tomatoes with the onions and garlic. Top these with the zucchini, then top the zucchini with the lettuce. Top the lettuce with the peas and sprinkle half the parsley and all the basil over the peas. Add the beans and sprinkle the remaining ½ cup parsley over the vegetables. (Make neat layers, covering each vegetable with the next as closely as possible.) Sprinkle the olive oil over everything. *Be sure to follow this order and do not stir or mix the vegetables.*

Cook, covered, over low to medium heat for 10 minutes, or until the vegetables start releasing their liquid. At this point, add salt and pepper to taste, reduce the heat to low, and stir and mix vegetables well. Cook, over low heat, covered, for about 20 to 30 minutes, stirring frequently, until tender but not mushy; do not overcook. Do not add water; the vegetables have enough moisture of their own. Serve hot, lukewarm, or at room temperature, but do not chill. Pass the grated cheese separately.

WATERCRESS AND PARSLEY SOUP

About 2 quarts (8 cups)

6 cups veal bouillon (see page 45), chicken bouillon, or water
2 medium potatoes, peeled and thinly sliced
1 small onion, thinly sliced
2 bunches watercress
1 cup loosely packed parsley, heads only
½ cup heavy cream
  Salt
  Freshly ground white pepper

In a large saucepan, combine the veal bouillon, potatoes, and onion. Bring to a boil. Reduce the heat, cover, and cook for about 20 minutes, or until potatoes and onions are tender. Purée in a blender or food processor until smooth. Return mixture to saucepan and heat through. In a food processor or by hand, very finely chop together the watercress and parsley, adding a little veal bouillon or water. Add watercress-parsley mixture to veal bouillon-potato mixture. Stir in the cream. Season with salt and pepper, to taste. Heat until very hot, but do not let boil. (If mixture boils, soup will lose its delicate green color and much of its flavor.)

COLD TARRAGON SOUP

About 2 quarts (8 cups)

¼ cup olive oil
4 medium cucumbers, about 7 to 8 inches long, peeled, seeded, and diced
6 cups chicken bouillon
3 tablespoons fresh or 1 tablespoon dried tarragon
Salt
Freshly ground pepper
½ cup heavy cream
1 tablespoon minced parsley or fresh tarragon

In a large saucepan, heat the olive oil. Add cucumbers and cook over medium heat for about 3 to 5 minutes, stirring occasionally. Add the chicken bouillon and tarragon. Cover and simmer cucumbers for about 25 minutes, or until tender. Purée small amounts of the broth-cucumber mixture in a blender or food processor until smooth. Pour into a large bowl. Season with salt and pepper to taste. Chill several hours or until very cold. Just before serving, stir in the cream. Garnish each serving with the parsley or tarragon.

CREAMY WATERCRESS SOUP

Good hot or chilled.

About 1 quart (4 cups)

1 bunch watercress
2 cups chicken bouillon
3 tablespoons cornstarch
6 tablespoons water
1 cup light or heavy cream
  Salt
  Freshly ground pepper
2 to 4 tablespoons Cognac
1 tablespoon butter (optional)

Wash the watercress and remove the bad leaves and any stems that are tough. Put the watercress and bouillon in a casserole. Bring to a boil, reduce the heat, and simmer for 5 minutes. Combine the cornstarch with the water to make a smooth mixture. Stir it gradually into the watercress soup. Remove from heat and purée in a blender or food processor to desired smoothness. Return the soup to the saucepan and stir in the cream. Season with salt and pepper to taste, and add the Cognac. Return to low heat and cook just long enough to heat through, but do not let boil. Remove from heat and stir in the butter if desired. Serve hot or chilled.

Eggs, Cheese, and Cereals

Eggs, cheese, and cereals are grouped together in one chapter because they are basic foods that complement one another. Either singly or in combination, they are easy meal makers that need only a little salad and/or fruit to create light, merry lunches, dinners, or suppers. They are basically nutritious, providing all the essentials, including carbohydrates, fiber, vitamins, and minerals. And they are a pleasure to cook and to eat. Besides, when you are at wit's end as to what to cook, think of the three steady faithfuls: eggs, cheese, and cereals. I do hope you have them always on hand. As you will see, mankind has long relied on this trio of foods.

"To make an omelet, you must break the eggs," says the French proverb. This saying has different levels of meaning, for the egg has always been not only a food but a symbol of life itself. In the Egyptian *Book of the Dead*, a passage speaks of "that great and glorious god in his egg, who created himself for that which came forth from him." In India there is the "cosmic egg" of Brahmanic tradition, and the Buddha used the symbol of the egg in one of his parables on spiritual rebirth. The egg was held sacred in ancient Greece's Orphic mysteries, and it appears in the North American myth of Hiawatha. The Romans also believed in the mystical power of eggs.

The Empress Livia, who wanted to know whether she was carrying a male or female child, was told by a seeress to place in her breast a newly laid egg until it hatched. If it brought forth a cockerel, the gods would grant Livia a son. This she did, and that is what happened. In due time she produced Tiberius, who, on becoming emperor proved himself capable by virtue of industry and application.

Eggs are a universal food, and though there are literally thousands of ways of serving them, there are only about six methods of cooking them. That is, eggs are either boiled, poached, scrambled, baked, fried, or cooked with other foods. All good cookbooks list many wonderful ways of cooking eggs; André Simon, in his *Concise Encyclopaedia of Gastronomy*, has some 240. Nevertheless, with the exception of omelets, Americans regard eggs as breakfast food. This is regrettable, since eggs are among the cheapest, most nourishing, and most palatable foods.

In this book I have listed some recipes that lend themselves to luncheons and suppers, because dishes of this kind are a great convenience either as entrées or as pre-entrée courses.

Eggs are one of nature's miracle foods; cheese is a man-made but no less miraculous food. It seems to me that mankind has always known that cheese was nutritious, and that people can get their protein and calcium from it. From my school days I remember that the Roman chronicler Pliny described Zoroaster, the Persian philosopher of the sixth century B.C., as having lived on nothing but cheese for twenty years. The Romans introduced cheese throughout their empire, and the great monasteries of the Middle Ages were famous cheese making centers.

Today cheese is fashionable, especially the more esoteric kinds of cheese. France has stolen the march on fancy cheeses, and Italy is now following. Oddly enough, the United States' cheese industry has not kept pace with our mania for new kinds of cheese, except for goat cheese. Dodging the brickbats, I maintain that *all* goat cheese, French, Italian, or American, tastes just like goat cheese—either fresh and mild, or older and strong.

I cook with cheese very frequently and can only pass on my mother's advice to me when I was young: "When you don't know what to cook, do something with cheese. It makes good starters for a meal. And when you serve cheese, take it out of the refrigerator in time so that it won't be stone cold." Also, "Don't bother to serve more than two or three different cheeses at your meal. People have already eaten their main dish, and it would be a waste of good cheese."

Among the fruits of the field, it is the grains that chiefly sustain life. They need not be consumed immediately, they can be stored against need, and in themselves they bear the seed of their renewal. Small wonder then that the religions of the world hold the grains in mystical reverence. Wheat and barley are perhaps the oldest grains known to civilized man of the Western World, and their place of origin is said to have been the fertile plains of the Euphrates from which they spread east and west.

Bread is the staff of life, the Bible tells us, and the Christian mass centers around bread and wine as divine symbols. In ancient Egypt, Greece, and Rome, and even in older civilizations, rites were celebrated to honor specific grains.

Demeter, the Greek goddess of the fields and fertility (the Romans knew her as Ceres, hence the word "cereal"), was at the heart of the Eleusinian mysteries, the secret cult that has been called the fountainhead of Greek culture. She is shown in ancient friezes holding sheaves of wheat, and to the hero Triptolemus the goddess gave the first grain, bidding him diffuse its blessing throughout the world. Chinese mythology tells of Shen-nung, the divine husbandman, who taught the Chinese the use of the plow and hoe so that they might cultivate millet and rice, the chief grains of China. On our own continent, the religious ceremonies of the Indians are intrinsically tied up with the mythology of corn, or maize, the life-sustaining cereal of the Americas.

From these cursory notes, we can see that the cult of the grain existed wherever civilization dawned. To pray for one's daily bread is indeed innate in man all over the earth.

BASQUE SCRAMBLED EGGS

PIPÉRADE

A delicious way of cooking eggs with tomatoes and vegetables, and very easy. In the Basque country pipérade *is served with ham, and a flavorful Smithfield ham or Italian prosciutto would go well with it. Be sure to serve plenty of crusty bread.* Pipérade *is never made with butter.*

Serves 4

⅓ cup lard or bacon fat
4 medium onions, thinly sliced
4 medium tomatoes, peeled and coarsely chopped
3 large or 5 small sweet peppers, green or red, cored, seeded, and sliced
 Salt
 Freshly ground pepper
¼ teaspoon dried thyme or marjoram
6 to 8 eggs, beaten

Melt the lard in a heavy skillet. Cook the onions over low heat for 5 to 10 minutes, or until very soft. They must not brown. Add the tomatoes, peppers, salt and pepper to taste, and the thyme. Cover and cook over very low heat for about 15 minutes, or until the vegetables are almost a purée, stirring frequently. Pour the beaten eggs into the vegetables and scramble gently with a fork until eggs are just set. The *pipérade* must be very soft. Serve very hot.

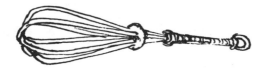

FARMERS' BREAKFAST

A good dish for luncheon or supper when you don't know what to cook.

Serves 2

6 slices bacon, cut crosswise into small strips
1 small sweet green pepper, cored, seeded, and diced
2 tablespoons finely chopped onion
3 large boiled potatoes, peeled and cubed (2 to 3 cups)
  Salt
  Freshly ground pepper
½ cup of any grated cheese
6 eggs

Fry the bacon over low heat until slightly browned and crisp. Drain off all but 3 tablespoons of fat. Add the green pepper, onion, potatoes, and salt and pepper to taste. Cook over medium heat for about 5 minutes, or until potatoes are golden, stirring frequently. Sprinkle the cheese over vegetables and stir. Break the eggs into pan over mixture and cook over low heat until eggs are set, stirring constantly. Do not beat the eggs beforehand. Serve with a green vegetable such as string beans or broccoli vinaigrette, or with a tossed green salad.

FRENCH POACHED EGGS IN RED WINE

It may seem strange at first to poach eggs in wine, but it is a surprisingly good way, and one that gives a little éclat to a luncheon.

Serves 3

1 cup dry red wine
1 cup chicken or beef bouillon
1 medium onion, sliced
1 clove garlic
  Salt
  Freshly ground pepper
⅛ teaspoon ground nutmeg
6 eggs
1½ tablespoons flour
1 tablespoon butter

Combine the wine, bouillon, onion, and garlic. Season with salt and pepper to taste, and add the nutmeg. Simmer, covered, over low heat for 10 minutes. Strain and return to a boil. Poach the eggs in wine-bouillon mixture. Remove eggs from liquid and keep hot. Boil liquid until it is reduced to 1 cup. Mix the flour and butter to a paste and add, a little at a time, to the hot liquid, stirring constantly. Serve eggs either on a hot purée of kidney beans or on slices of toast buttered on one side only, placing the eggs on the unbuttered side to prevent them from sliding off the bread. Pour reduced poaching liquid over eggs and serve immediately.

FRENCH BAKED EGGS AND ONIONS

Serves 3

6 tablespoons butter
2 large onions, thinly sliced
6 hard-boiled eggs, sliced
  Salt
  Cayenne pepper
2 tablespoons flour
1⅔ cups hot light cream
1 teaspoon Dijon mustard
2 tablespoons grated Swiss or Parmesan cheese
1 egg yolk
2 tablespoons milk

Heat 4 tablespoons of the butter, but do not let it brown. Cook the onions over medium heat for 5 to 7 minutes, or until soft. The onions must remain pale. Butter a shallow baking dish. Arrange alternate layers of hard-boiled eggs and onions. Sprinkle with salt to taste and a little cayenne pepper.

Melt the remaining 2 tablespoons butter and stir in the flour. Blend in the hot cream and cook over medium heat until sauce is thickened, stirring constantly. Add the mustard and cheese, and cook for 2 to 3 minutes longer. Beat together the egg yolk and milk. Remove cheese sauce from heat and stir in egg yolk mixture. Pour sauce over hard-boiled eggs and onions, and broil quickly until top is brown and bubbly. Or bake in hot (425° F) oven. (The broiler method is better, however, since it will not dry out the dish.) Serve with Garbanzos Fritos and a tomato salad.

CURRIED EGGS AU GRATIN

In French cooking, curry powder is used as a flavoring rather than as a chief ingredient as in Indian cooking. Serve for lunch or supper with a green vegetable or a tossed salad.

Serves 4

6 hard-boiled eggs, cut in half lengthwise
¼ cup butter
2 tablespoons flour
1 cup milk
⅓ cup heavy cream or crème fraîche
1 tablespoon sour cream
2 teaspoons curry powder
Salt
Freshly ground pepper

With a demitasse spoon, carefully scoop out the yolks from the hard-boiled egg halves and put them into a small bowl. Generously butter an 8-inch shallow baking dish that can go to the table; I use a round, scalloped white French one. Place the egg halves neatly into the baking dish. With a fork, mash the yolks until smooth or whirl them in a food processor. Reserve.

Preheat the oven to hot (425° F). Heat the butter in a saucepan and stir in the flour. Stir until smooth. Remove from heat and gradually stir in the milk, stirring constantly to avoid lumping. Return to low heat. Cook, stirring constantly, for about 7 minutes, until thick and smooth; this long stirring and cooking is necessary to remove any raw flour taste. Remove from heat and stir in the cream or crème fraîche; if heavy cream is used, stir in the sour cream. Mix thoroughly. Stir in the curry powder and season with salt and pepper to taste. Add the mashed egg yolks to the sauce and blend well. Spoon a little of this mixture into each egg half and top the stuffed eggs with the remaining sauce. Bake for 10 minutes, or until browned and bubbly. Serve immediately from the dish.

RAGOUT OF MUSHROOMS AND EGGS

Serve as an entrée, or with ham or sausages.

Serves 3

- 2 tablespoons olive oil
- 1 tablespoon minced onion
- 1 tablespoon chopped parsley
- 1 pound mushrooms, sliced
- 1 tablespoon flour
- ½ cup dry white wine
- Salt
- Freshly ground pepper
- 6 hard-boiled eggs, coarsely chopped

Heat the olive oil over medium heat, and cook the onion and parsley for 2 minutes. Add the mushrooms and cook, covered, over low heat for 10 minutes. Stir in the flour and add the wine. Cover and simmer for 5 minutes. Season with salt and pepper to taste. Add the eggs and simmer, covered, for 5 more minutes, stirring occasionally.

FRIED EGGS SOUBISE

Quickly made and good for brunch, lunch, or a late supper.

Serves 1

2 tablespoons butter
2 to 3 medium onions, thinly sliced
2 eggs
Salt
Freshly ground pepper

Heat the butter in an individual shallow flameproof dish. Cook the onions on top of the stove, over low heat, stirring frequently, until soft and golden. Make 2 indentations. Break an egg into each. Season with salt and pepper to taste. Cover and cook over low heat until the eggs are set and the yolk is covered with a thin film. Serve immediately with crisp toast or French bread.

NOTE: Be sure to use a flameproof dish to prevent the dish from cracking over the direct heat. If necessary, use a "flametamer" or other top-of-the-stove heat-retarding gadget.

SPANISH EGGS BAKED À LA FLAMENCA

Serves 4

- 3 tablespoons butter
- 1 large onion, sliced
- ¼ pound ham, diced
- 1 clove garlic, minced
- 3 medium tomatoes, peeled and chopped
- 1 cup cooked peas
- 1 cup cooked string beans, cut into 1-inch pieces
- 1 tablespoon chopped parsley
- ⅓ cup chopped pimiento-stuffed olives
  Salt
  Freshly ground pepper
- 4 eggs

Preheat the oven to moderate (350° F).

Melt the butter in a medium saucepan or a large, deep frying pan. Add the onion, ham, and garlic, and cook over medium heat until onion is tender, stirring occasionally. Add the tomatoes and cook for 10 minutes. Add the peas, beans, parsley, and olives, season with salt and pepper to taste, and mix well. Turn into 4 individual baking dishes. Break an egg over each dish. Bake for 20 minutes, or until eggs are set. Serve as a first dinner course, or, with some good bread, for lunch.

SWISS EGGS

Very simple and very good, especially for brunch.

Serves 4

1 pound Swiss cheese, sliced
8 eggs
Salt
Freshly ground pepper
⅔ cup heavy cream
⅓ cup grated Swiss cheese

Preheat the oven to moderate (350° F).

Heavily butter the bottom of a shallow baking dish. Line with the sliced cheese. Break the eggs over cheese. Season with salt and pepper to taste. Pour the cream over eggs. Sprinkle with the grated cheese. Bake for 15 minutes, or until set.

BRIE EN CROUTE

When you serve this as the cheese course, you need not serve bread or crackers with the cheese. The pastry should be fresh and crisp.

Serves 16 to 20

1 10-ounce package frozen patty shells, thawed
1 whole Brie cheese (about 2½ pounds), about 8 inches in diameter
1 egg, beaten

Preheat the oven to moderate (375° F).

Stack 4 of the patty shells on a work surface and pinch edges together. Roll out into a 10½-inch circle (or a circle equal to the diameter of Brie plus twice the height of the cheese plus ½ inch for overlap). Place the Brie in the middle of the circle. Stack the 2 remaining patty shells and pinch edges together. Roll out into an 8-inch circle. Place on top of Brie, then bring up bottom circle edge to top circle edge. Firmly pinch edges together with fingers to completely encase cheese. Carefully place pastry-enclosed Brie, seam side down, on a large ungreased baking sheet. Brush the top and side with some of the beaten egg. Bake for 25 to 30 minutes, or until golden brown. During baking, if pastry puffs up too much, prick *pastry only* with toothpick or cake tester to allow air to escape. Do not prick Brie as it may run out. Remove to a wire rack and allow to cool to room temperature. Cut into wedges. The Brie will have turned a color that is closer to that of Gouda, somewhat yellow, losing its familiar whitish-yellow color.

PETITS PAINS AU BRIE

I had this in France as the cheese course.

Serves 6 (about 2⅓ cups sauce)

- 3 tablespoons butter, at room temperature
- 12 slices Italian or French bread
  Paprika
- 2 tablespoons minced shallots (about 3 medium)
- 1 cup heavy cream
- ½ cup puréed or firmly packed very finely chopped cooked ham
- ¾ pound firm Brie cheese, white part scraped off with knife, cut into small pieces
- 1 tablespoon brandy
  Salt
  Freshly ground pepper
  Cayenne pepper

Preheat the oven to low (250° to 275° F).

Using 2 tablespoons of the butter, butter 1 side of the bread slices. Sprinkle the buttered side lightly with paprika. Place on a baking sheet and bake until hot and slightly toasted.

In a saucepan, heat the remaining tablespoon butter until melted. Add the shallots and cook for about 2 to 3 minutes, or until just tender, stirring frequently. Add the cream and bring to a boil. Boil gently until mixture is reduced to ⅔ cup, about 4 minutes. Stir in the ham. Add the Brie. Cook over low heat, stirring constantly, until mixture is smooth and hot; do not boil. Stir in the brandy. Season with salt, ground pepper, and cayenne pepper to taste. Spoon cheese mixture over warm bread slices.

CHEESE BALLS

Serves 4 or 5 (about 18 balls)

½ cup grated very sharp Cheddar cheese
½ cup butter
¼ teaspoon Worcestershire sauce
  About 1 cup flour

Cream the cheese and butter together until soft. Blend in the Worcestershire sauce. Gradually add the flour, mixing until a soft dough is formed. Chill for 30 minutes to 1 hour.

Preheat the oven to hot (425° F). Roll dough into small balls the size of smallish cherry tomatoes. Place on a lightly greased baking sheet. Bake for 10 minutes, or until golden. Serve hot, wrapped in a napkin, as an hors d'oeuvre or to accompany soup.

DEVIL'S KISSES OR FRIED CHEESE BALLS

Serves 6 (about 24 balls)

Oil for deep-frying (preferably peanut)
3 large egg whites
Salt
Freshly ground pepper
3 cups grated gruyère cheese (8 to 9 ounces)
½ cup fresh fine dry bread crumbs

Pour oil into a large saucepan or deep fryer, to a depth of 3 inches, and heat. In a small bowl, using an electric beater at low speed, beat egg whites with a dash of salt and pepper until foamy. Gradually increase speed to high and beat until egg whites are stiff. Fold in the cheese. Shape mixture into small balls, using a generous teaspoon for each ball. Coat balls with the bread crumbs, pressing crumbs onto surface of balls. Drop several balls at a time into the hot (357° F) oil and fry until golden brown, about 2 minutes, turning if necessary. Remove with a slotted spoon and drain on paper towels. Repeat with remaining balls. Serve hot as an hors d'oeuvre or for a cheese course with cheese crackers.

NOTE: You may shape the balls using 2 teaspoons rinsed in cold water and shaken dry. Or use your hands, rinsed in cold water and shaken dry.

You may use the usual breadcube test—drop a small cube of bread in the oil; if it turns brown in a few seconds the oil is hot enough.

MASCOTTE

Betty Boulpaep's cheese patties.

Serves 4

4 frozen patty shells (from 1 10-ounce package frozen patty shells) baked according to package directions
¼ cup butter
½ cup flour
1 cup milk
1¼ cups grated gruyère cheese
Salt
Freshly ground pepper
Ground nutmeg
1 large egg yolk, lightly beaten

Preheat the oven to low (300° F).

In a small saucepan, heat the butter until melted. Stir in the flour. Cook and stir over low heat until mixture comes to a boil and thickens. (Mixture will be very thick.) Add 1 cup of the cheese. Using a wooden spoon, stir until cheese is melted. Season with salt, pepper, and nutmeg to taste. Cool briefly. Beat in the egg yolk. Place baked patty shells on a lightly greased baking sheet; remove and reserve the tops. Fill patty shells with cheese mixture using about ⅓ cup for each shell. Sprinkle the remaining ¼ cup cheese over filled shells. Sprinkle lightly with nutmeg. Top with pastry shell top, then bake for about 10 minutes, or just until filling is hot in center. (Or, if desired, freeze. To reheat, bake in preheated moderate [300° F] oven until filling is hot in center, about 20 to 25 minutes.) Serve as a cheese course, a hot hors d'oeuvre, or as a light luncheon dish with a salad.

NOTE: The cheese filling has to be very thick or it will run out of the patties in baking.

DEEP-FRIED MEDALLIONS OF MOZZARELLA

This is Italian home cookery.

Serves 6 (27 pieces)

1 1-pound package mozzarella cheese
¼ cup flour
2 large eggs, well beaten
1 cup fine dry bread crumbs
   Oil for deep-frying (preferably peanut)

With a sharp knife, cut the cheese lengthwise into 9 slices, each slice about ½ inch thick. Then cut each slice crosswise into thirds. Pieces of cheese will measure approximately 1¼ x 1¾ inches. Roll each piece of cheese in the flour, then dip in the beaten eggs. Roll in the bread crumbs until cheese pieces are thoroughly coated. Chill until ready to serve. To serve, deep-fry cheese pieces, a few at a time, in deep hot (375° F) oil until golden brown, about 1 minute. Drain on paper towels. Serve hot as a first course. For a light lunch or supper, serve with a green vegetable or tossed salad.

QUICHE LORRAINE

Quiche is not as fashionable a dish as it was a few years ago, but it still tastes as good and is a most convenient thing to make when you don't know what to cook and serve. Since I prefer quiche Lorraine to all others, I recommend this simple recipe.

Serves 4 to 6

3 eggs, beaten
1 cup light cream, half and half, or half milk, half heavy cream
6 slices crisply cooked bacon, crumbled
2 tablespoons Dijon mustard
¼ cup minced onion
1 cup grated Swiss cheese
  Salt
  Freshly ground pepper
1 unbaked 9-inch pie shell, set in a 9-inch pie plate

Preheat the oven to moderate (375° F).

Combine all the ingredients except the pie shell and mix well. Turn into the pie shell. Bake for 35 minutes, or until a knife inserted into the filling tests clean. Let stand at room temperature for 3 to 4 minutes before cutting and serving.

YOGURT CHEESE

This yogurt cheese resembles cream cheese or ricotta, but without the richness of those two cheeses. It is absolutely delicious used whenever you would use cream cheese or ricotta. Serve it with jam, guava paste, or any jelly and crackers for a snack or dessert. It's low in calories too—1 cup has about 270 calories.

1 cup

2 cups plain yogurt (can be low-fat yogurt)

Line a sieve or strainer with a double layer of cheesecloth. Turn the yogurt into the strainer. Set strainer over a bowl and let stand at room temperature for about 30 to 45 minutes, to drain off liquid. Tie the corners of the cheesecloth together to form a bag. Tie the bag to the faucet over the sink by wrapping a string around the top and fastening it to the neck of the faucet. Or suspend the bag from a heavy skewer and set it over a deep bowl. Let the yogurt drain for at least 12 hours, or until it has turned into a firm and dry cheese. (I do this after I've done the supper dishes and let the yogurt drain overnight in the sink.) Untie the bag and turn the yogurt cheese into a bowl. (The cheesecloth can be washed and used again and again.) Refrigerate, covered, for up to 10 days.

BARLEY CASSEROLE

Barley is much eaten in Eastern European countries such as Poland, and it deserves to come to the American table in lieu of potatoes and other starches. Americans have mostly relegated it to soup, yet it is excellent with meats, such as lamb, and with poultry. Once the basic preparation is mastered, and very easy it is, too, any number of variations can be worked with sautéed chicken livers, herb seasonings, cottage cheese, or sour cream, which are mixed with the cooked barley. Fine or medium pearl barleys are best, since the kernels swell.

Serves 4 to 6

¼ cup butter or bacon fat
1 medium onion, chopped
½ pound mushrooms, sliced (optional)
1 cup pearl barley
2 cups boiling chicken or beef bouillon

Heat the butter in a heavy saucepan. Add the onion and sauté over medium heat for 3 to 4 minutes, or until golden, stirring constantly. Do not brown. Add the mushrooms, if used, and cook for 5 minutes longer. Add the barley and cook over medium heat for 5 minutes, or until it just begins to brown. Pour the boiling bouillon over barley. Cover tightly and cook over lowest possible heat for about 25 minutes, or until barley is tender, each grain separate, and all the liquid is absorbed. If casserole is too liquid, cook uncovered to allow for evaporation. Conversely, add more bouillon, a little at a time, if the casserole is too dry.

NOTE: Chopped toasted almonds (about ½ cup) can be mixed into the cooked barley. Or use more mushrooms. Or sauté ½ pound chicken livers and add to casserole.

RICE PILAFF

How nice
Is Rice!
How gentle, and how very free from vice
Are those whose fodder is mainly Rice!
Rice! Rice!
Really it doesn't want thinking of twice:
The gambler would quickly abandon his dice,
The criminal classes be quiet as mice,
If carefully fed upon nothing but Rice.
Yes; Rice! Rice!
Beautiful Rice!
All the wrong in the world would be right in a trice
If everyone fed upon nothing but Rice.

This poem comes from a charming book by the late André Simon, entitled Food, *in the Pleasures of Life series (Burke Publishing Company Ltd, 1949). I am very fond of it, particularly because the anonymous author disregarded the fact that rice-eating people are anything but quiet mice. The Greeks, the Turks, the Arabs, the Chinese and Japanese, rice-eaters all, may be free from vice—depending on how one looks upon vice—but gentle they are not. Yet the Greeks, Turks, and the people of the Balkans are among the most hospitable and noble, if ruthless, in their approach to many aspects of life. I remember reading that a long time ago a visitor to Turkey expressed his opinion on pilaff this way: "They put before you fortie dishes called by fortie names as Pelo, chelo, etc., albeit indeed it differ but thus all are of ryce, mutton and hens boyl'd together. Some have butter, some have none, some have termerick and saffron, some have none; some have onions and garlic, some have none, some have almonds and raisins, some have none, and so on ad infinitum."*

PLAIN PILAFF

Know your rice when you make pilaff. Cooked converted rice makes for grains that are firmer than those of other kinds of cooked rice; in pilaff I prefer it to the usual long-grain rice. But this is a matter of taste. The different kinds of rice require somewhat different amounts of liquid in their cooking; look at package directions and experiment. Remember, pilaff is a dry rice dish.

Serves 4 to 6

¼ cup butter or other fat
2 cups rice
2 cups boiling chicken or other bouillon
　 Salt
　 Freshly ground pepper

Melt the butter in a heavy saucepan. Sauté the rice over medium heat 3 to 5 minutes; stirring constantly, until golden and transparent. Pour in the boiling bouillon; the rice will sizzle in an alarming manner. Cover tightly (the Middle Easterners cover the pan with a cloth before putting on the lid) and cook over lowest possible heat for about 20 to 25 minutes, or until the rice is just tender and all the liquid has been absorbed. Season with salt and pepper to taste. Keep the rice hot for 5 to 10 minutes before serving. This is not absolutely necessary, but it improves the pilaff. It can be done by standing the rice on the warm stove, wrapping a cloth around the pan, or keeping it in a warm oven. Serve with roasted meats instead of potatoes, or as the starch of a vegetarian meal.

CHICKEN PILAFF FROM THE BALKANS

Serves 6 to 8

½ cup butter
2 tablespoons finely minced onion
2 cups raw or cooked chicken, lamb, or rabbit, cut into thin strips
Salt
Freshly ground pepper
¼ teaspoon dried thyme
2 cups rice
4 cups boiling chicken bouillon
2 medium tomatoes, peeled, seeded, and chopped
¼ cup coarsely chopped walnuts

Melt the butter in a heavy saucepan. Cook the onion over low heat for about 3 minutes, or until golden. Add the chicken and cook for 3 minutes longer. Season with salt and pepper to taste, and add the thyme. Add the rice and cook over medium heat for 5 minutes, stirring constantly. Pour in the boiling bouillon, and add the tomatoes and walnuts. Cover tightly and cook over lowest possible heat for about 20 minutes, or until all the liquid has been absorbed. Serve as a main dish with a side dish of plain yogurt.

PILAFF OF RICE WITH RAISINS AND PINE NUTS

Shredded or slivered blanched almonds may be substituted for the pine nuts, and dark raisins for the golden ones. But the golden ones make for a nicer-looking dish. Serve with a buttered green vegetable for a meatless meal.

Serves 8

3 tablespoons butter
1 cup pine nuts
3 cups rice, preferably converted rice
  About 5 cups boiling chicken or beef bouillon
1 cup dry white wine
1 cup golden raisins
  Salt
  Freshly ground pepper

Heat the butter in a heavy casserole. Cook the pine nuts and rice over medium heat, stirring constantly, for about 3 minutes, or until the rice is opaque and the pine nuts barely golden. Pour in the boiling bouillon and the wine; the dish will sizzle. Reduce the heat to very low. Add the raisins. Simmer, covered, for about 15 to 20 minutes, or until the rice is tender but still firm. After 10 minutes, season with salt and pepper to taste. If the rice shows any signs of possible scorching, add a little more boiling bouillon, about 2 tablespoons at a time, stirring after each addition. When the rice is cooked, turn off the heat, fold a kitchen towel to the size of the casserole, and lay it over the rice. Cover with the lid and let stand for 5 to 10 minutes before serving. This will absorb excess moisture and leave the rice dry, as it should be. Remove the towel before serving from the casserole.

SAVORY PILAFF

A wonderful party dish, using leftover meats in any desired combination. The amounts can easily be doubled or tripled with perfect success, provided the pan used is large enough.

Serves 6 to 8

½ cup butter
3 medium onions, finely chopped
½ pound cold roast beef or lamb, cut into 1 x 2-inch strips
⅓ cup pine nuts
⅓ cup currants or raisins, plumped in water
2 cups rice
4 cups boiling chicken or beef bouillon
2 large tomatoes, peeled, seeded, and chopped
2 tablespoons chopped parsley
1 teaspoon powdered sage
½ teaspoon ground coriander, or more to taste
¼ teaspoon ground cinnamon

Heat the butter in a large heavy kettle. Sauté the onions over low heat for 5 minutes, or until golden. They must not brown. Add the beef strips and cook for 3 minutes. Add the pine nuts and currants, and cook for 3 minutes longer, stirring constantly. Add the rice and cook for 5 minutes over medium heat, stirring constantly. Pour in the boiling bouillon, and add the tomatoes, parsley, sage, coriander, and cinnamon. Mix thoroughly. Cover tightly and cook over lowest possible heat for about 20 minutes, or until rice is tender. If possible, let stand, covered, in a warm place for 10 minutes before serving.

RICE TIMBALE

A handsome and ornamental creation of Milanese cooking, well suited to buffet suppers or for show-off dinners.

Serves 8

2⅔ cups Carolina or Italian Arborio rice
½ cup butter
⅓ cup freshly grated Parmesan cheese
4 egg yolks
Fine bread crumbs
Filling (see below)

Preheat the oven to moderate (350° F).

Cook the rice in plenty of boiling salted water until tender. Drain. Mix in the butter, the cheese, and the egg yolks. Butter a 3-quart casserole and sprinkle with fine dry bread crumbs. (The casserole must be thoroughly coated.) Spoon two thirds of the rice mixture into the casserole. Press rice against bottom and sides, leaving a well in the middle. Put filling in the well. Spoon the remaining rice over the top of the entire casserole, taking care that the meat is well covered. Bake for about 1 hour, or until rice is set. Unmold on a heated platter. Cut into wedges and serve with a plain tomato sauce.

FILLING:
2 tablespoons butter
¼ cup finely minced onion
1 clove garlic, finely minced
1 pound mixed veal and pork, ground twice
½ pound chicken livers, trimmed and chopped
⅓ cup minced pimiento
1½ cups cooked peas
4 tablespoons Italian-style tomato paste flavored with basil
1 teaspoon salt
1 teaspoon sugar
½ teaspoon dried oregano
¼ teaspoon freshly ground pepper

Melt the butter in a skillet. Sauté the onion and garlic over low heat until onion is golden and transparent. Add the ground meat and chicken livers. Cook, stirring occasionally, for about 15 minutes, or until meats are brown but not dried out. Add the pimiento, peas, tomato paste, salt, sugar, oregano, and pepper. Cook over low heat for about 20 minutes, stirring frequently. The mixture should be thick.

COUNTRY RISOTTO

This is a kind of catch-all recipe, where you can substitute whatever you have on hand for the vegetables listed—limas instead of peas, parsnip instead of turnip, etc. But try to keep the proportions and the sage flavoring, though that too can be replaced with a favorite herb. The dish is really a vegetable stew, and if your family clamors for meat, simply add some frankfurters or sliced sausage to it for the last 20 minutes. Or add leftover chicken, cut into bite-size pieces, for the last 10 minutes.

Serves 6

  1 cup dry white navy beans
3½ cups chicken or beef bouillon
  2 medium potatoes, peeled and cut into ½-inch cubes
  2 large carrots, sliced
  2 medium artichokes, thinly sliced (see below) or 1 9- or 10-ounce package frozen artichoke hearts, thawed and cut in half
  2 large zucchini, thinly sliced
  2 leeks, white and green parts, sliced, or 1 bunch green onions, white and green parts, sliced
  1 turnip, cut into ½-inch cubes
  1 cup long-grain rice
  1 10-ounce package frozen peas, thawed
    Salt
    Freshly ground pepper
 ¾ teaspoon ground sage
 ½ cup melted butter
    Freshly grated Parmesan cheese

Wash the beans, put them into a bowl, and add enough boiling water to cover beans by 2 inches. Let stand for 1 hour, then drain. Put the beans into a deep kettle, add cold water to cover, and cook, covered, over low heat for about 40 minutes. The beans must be almost tender and keep their shape. Add 3 cups of the bouillon and bring to a boil. Add the potatoes, carrots, artichokes, zucchini, leeks, and turnip. Cook, uncovered, over high heat for about 4 minutes, stirring frequently but carefully so as not to break the vegetables. Add the rice and the remaining ½ cup bouillon. Cook, covered, over medium heat, stirring frequently, until the rice is almost tender. Add the peas, and season with salt and pepper to taste. Cook, covered, for about 10 minutes, or until rice and peas are tender. If risotto is too liquid, cook without a cover to reduce the liquid. If too thick, add a little more bouillon or hot water, 2 tablespoons at a time. Stir the sage into the butter and stir into the risotto. Serve hot or lukewarm, but not cold. Pass the grated cheese separately.

ARTICHOKES
Strip off tough outer leaves of each artichoke, cut off spiky tips, and quarter each artichoke as you would quarter an apple. Remove the choke and slice the quarters, dropping them as they are ready into cold water with a little vinegar or lemon juice (2 tablespoons to 1 quart water) to prevent discoloration. Keep pieces submerged in acidulated water until ready to use, then drain.

NOTE: I bring this to the table in the casserole in which it was cooked—a deep, enameled French one that looks pretty and rustic on the table.

ORIGINAL NOODLES ALFREDO

The original Alfredo was an excellent restaurateur who ran a famous restaurant in the old Roman street via della Scrofa—*the Street of the Sow (the sow appears on an antique frieze that used to be there). Alfredo was a born ham, and his customers loved it. He used to celebrate this noodle dish—there is no other word for his technique—with a golden spoon and fork, tossing the noodles with a flourish.*

The noodle dish is excellent even when made with "boughten" noodles. The trick is to use equal parts of noodles, butter, and freshly ground Parmesan cheese, and to have everything extremely hot. Also, the butter must not be melted. When made with first-class ingredients, this is one of the great noodle dishes of all time—and never mind the calories.

Serves 4

1 pound broad noodles (preferably homemade)
1 pound sweet butter (it *must* be sweet), cut into 1-inch slices, at room temperature
1 pound freshly grated Parmesan cheese (it must be freshly grated for this dish)
  Salt
  Freshly ground pepper

Cook the noodles al dente. Drain and put into a big, very hot bowl. Add the butter and cheese. Season with salt and pepper to taste. Toss very thoroughly so that the noodles are evenly coated. Serve immediately on very hot plates as a first course.

SPAGHETTI WITH FRESH PEAS

Serves 4 to 6

¼ pound Italian prosciutto or Canadian or other bacon, cut into pieces
1 medium onion, cut into quarters
1 clove garlic
1 3-inch piece celery
1 cup loosely packed parsley leaves
¼ cup olive oil
3 tablespoons butter
1½ pounds fresh peas, shelled
⅓ cup chicken bouillon
1 large tomato, peeled, seeded, and chopped
2 tablespoons minced fresh basil
   Salt
   Freshly ground pepper
1 pound pasta, such as spaghetti, linguine, or other
1 to 2 tablespoons butter
   Freshly grated Parmesan cheese

On a chopping board or in a food processor, mince together the proscuitto, onion, garlic, celery, and parsley. Heat together the olive oil and the 3 tablespoons of butter. Cook the prosciutto and vegetable mixture over low heat for about 5 minutes. Add the peas and bouillon. Cover and simmer until peas are tender, stirring occasionally. Toward the end of the cooking time, add the tomato and basil. Season with salt and pepper to taste. If there is too much liquid, cook uncovered to allow for evaporation. The mixture should be dry, not soupy.

While the mixture is cooking, cook in plenty of rapidly boiling salted water. Drain, and toss with the vegetable mixture and 1 to 2 tablespoons butter. Pass the grated cheese separately.

Fish

I have often speculated on the nature of the person who first thought of eating a lobster. How would it occur to one that any animal so clad in armor would be edible at all? And did this pioneer progress from lobster to shellfish or vice versa? Who knows, indeed?

Until recently, fish was one of the cheapest foods—there for the taking, so to speak. Now it is no longer thus and often even worse, at least in cities not on the sea. And even when near the sea or lake or stream, the fish available is no longer invariably as fresh as it should be to be worth eating. To my mind I think fish has to be absolutely and totally fresh, and I fail to see how it can be so in our age of scientific food preservation and public indifference to flavor. When fish smells fishy, I don't want it any longer. The fish markets of Norway proved to me that fish markets need not be as smelly as even our fanciest American fish markets tend to be. It is obvious that I am not a natural fish cook, especially since for myself I only like *fresh* fish that has been plainly boiled or broiled with no sauce but a little butter, or, if it must be, quickly pan-fried as in the case of fresh-caught mountain trout. In Norway, where the fish is really fresh and very firm, coming from the country's icy waters, I experienced plain fish cookery at its sublime heights. What especially impressed me in the houses where I dined was that the second helping of the fish dish was invariably freshly and newly cooked, as if it were the first offering. With it came freshly boiled potatoes, to my mind the only vegetable suited to fish—but I presume this is a matter of taste. I think that sauces, wonderful as they are, spoil the flavor of really fresh fish, but then I am not a sauce lover on anything. However, since most people do not agree with me, some of the recipes that follow are sauced. I have cooked them for friends who liked them and said they should get into this book. So be it, I say, leaving the choice of fish side dishes to you since, as I said, I don't approve of anything but boiled potatoes and if need be, a little plain buttered rice to sop up the sauces.

———

RUSSIAN OR POLISH COD WITH RED WINE AND CHERRIES

I once knew a very old Russian lady in Rome, an émigrée even poorer than most of them. She earned her few pennies doing embroidery for one of the tourist shops and starved most of the time. She had many friends, but she was as proud as Lucifer, and to get her to accept even a luncheon invitation involved Machiavellian skill. The most interesting thing about her was the way she lived, which made a deep impression on me as a child. A Roman princess, a friend of hers, had given her an enormous, high-ceilinged attic rent free in her palace, and here Madame X (she would not like me to use her real name, even though she is dead) camped. Literally, she camped. Since the attic was not heated and had a marble floor—marble being the cheapest flooring at the time the palace was built, in the sixteenth century—and since Roman winters can be very cold, Madame X had erected a small army tent in a corner of this gigantic room. There she sat in winter, huddled over a small charcoal brazier, doing her intricate stitches by the light of a small oil lamp, for it was dark in the tent. And there was nothing anybody could do about it. I remember being taken to see her often by my mother, who loved her. Madame X would give us glasses of tea, which we sucked through lumps of sugar, and flat fruit cookies that she called mazureks, *making the word sound like "mazurka," which surprised me every time, since I thought mazurkas were dances by Chopin.*

To come to the cod with cherries. Madame X could afford only the food of the poorest of the poor, and salt cod was as much a part of her diet as it was of other poor Romans. My mother detested salt cod over all things. But one day Madame X decided to return some of the hospitality shown her and invited several of her friends, including us, to lunch. The salt cod with cherries was the pièce de résistance, *and wonder of wonders, my mother liked it and asked for the recipe. I found it among my mother's things many years later, and curiosity prompted me to make it. My mother still liked it, and so did I. It is best made with fresh sour cherries, which are as cheap in Rome as cod, but canned sour cherries will do.*

I checked on the recipe and found that cooking cod this way is common practice in Russia and Poland, where they love sour dishes. But there it is made with fresh cod. Poor Madame X could not afford fresh fish, so she made with the salt cod what turned out to be a highly original and excellent dish.

When buying salt cod, one should choose fish that is white, not yellowish. The fish must always be desalted before cooking. But before desalting it, it is a good idea to give it a dozen or so good strong whacks against a table to break down the fibers, as they do in Italy. The best way of desalting cod is to leave it in running water overnight. If this is not convenient, soak in cold water for twenty-four hours, changing water at least six times. Desalted cod must never be boiled, a fact that is often overlooked; the result is tough, stringy fish. The liquid in which it cooks must barely simmer. Allow 1 pound of salt cod for 3 people.

Serves 6

---

2 pounds salt cod, soaked and desalted
2 cups milk, scalded
Boiling water

Cut the cod into bite-size pieces. Put cod into a saucepan and cover with the milk. Simmer, over very low heat for 10 to 15 minutes. Do not let boil. Drain, and pour boiling water over cod to wash off milk and drain again. Keep hot.

SAUCE

- 1 cup sour cherries, pitted and chopped
- 1⅔ cups water or chicken bouillon
- 2 tablespoons butter
- Sugar to taste (the sauce should be tart)
- ¼ teaspoon ground cinnamon
- ¼ teaspoon ground cloves
- 1 cup dry red wine
- 1 tablespoon cornstarch

Simmer the cherries, water, and butter over low heat for 5 minutes. Add the sugar, cinnamon, cloves, and wine. Simmer for 5 minutes longer. Mix the cornstarch with a little cold water. Bring sauce to a boil and stir in cornstarch. Reduce the heat and simmer until sauce is thickened and shiny, stirring constantly. Put cooked pieces of cod into sauce. Cover and simmer over low heat for 10 minutes. Serve with boiled rice.

COD PROVENÇALE

See my notes on salt cod on page 100.

Serves 4

1 pound salt cod
¼ cup flour
¼ cup olive oil
½ cup chopped onion
2 cloves garlic, crushed
2 28-ounce cans whole tomatoes, very well drained and chopped
   (3 cups), or about 6 medium tomatoes, peeled and chopped
¼ teaspoon dried rosemary, crumbled
¼ teaspoon ground sage
2 bay leaves
   Freshly ground pepper
   Chopped parsley (optional)

In a large saucepan or kettle, soak the cod in cold water to cover amply overnight; drain. Rinse well; drain again. Return cod to saucepan or kettle, cover with cold water, and bring to a boil. Reduce the heat and simmer just until fish barely flakes easily with a fork, about 10 to 15 minutes. Drain well. Pat cod dry with paper towels. Carefully dredge cod with the flour. Heat the olive oil in a large heavy frying pan. Add cod and cook over medium heat until lightly browned on both sides, about 10 to 15 minutes, turning once. Remove cod; set aside. Add onion to remaining oil and drippings in pan. Cook over medium heat for about 5 to 7 minutes, until tender, stirring occasionally. Stir in the garlic, tomatoes, rosemary, thyme, sage, and bay leaves, and add pepper to taste. Cover and simmer over low heat for about 30 minutes, stirring occasionally. Add cod. Simmer, uncovered for 15 to 20 minutes or until fish flakes easily with a fork and is heated through thoroughly. Garnish with parsley if desired.

LOW-CALORIE BAKED FISH

Serves 3 or 4

1½ pounds fillet of sole or other fish (if frozen, thawed and
     dried)
     Salt
     Freshly ground pepper
 ¾ cup dry vermouth
 ⅓ cup water
     Lemon wedges

Preheat the oven to moderate (350° F).

Butter a shallow ovenproof dish. Place the fish fillets in a single or double layer in the dish, and sprinkle with salt and pepper to taste. Combine the vermouth and water, and pour over the fish. Bake for 10 to 15 minutes, or until the fish flakes easily with a fork. Serve garnished with lemon wedges.

Fillets of Flounder in Cream

Serves 4 to 6

¼ cup minced shallots
2 pounds fillet of flounder (8 or 9 fillets), cut in half crosswise
 Salt
 Freshly ground pepper
¼ cup dry white wine
¼ cup heavy cream
2 tablespoons minced green onion (white part of 3 medium with some green part)

Preheat the oven to hot (400° F).

Butter the bottom of an oblong 3-quart glass casserole. Sprinkle the shallots evenly over bottom of casserole. Fold the fillets in half lengthwise, skin side in. Arrange fillets on bed of shallots. Season with salt and pepper to taste. Pour on the wine and cream. Bake for 10 to 15 minutes, or until fish flakes easily with a fork. Sprinkle fish with the green onions. Serve at once on heated plates.

HALIBUT WITH LEEKS

Serves 4

4 leeks, white part only, cut into 1-inch pieces (about 1 cup)
4 boneless halibut steaks (1¾ to 2 pounds), about 1 inch thick
  (see Note)
½ cup dry white wine
½ cup fish bouillon or water
1 tablespoon butter
2 tablespoons minced shallots
½ cup heavy cream
1 tablespoon fresh lemon juice
  Salt
  Freshly ground pepper
1 green onion, green part only, minced

Preheat the oven to hot (400° F).

Fill a small saucepan three-fourths full with water. Bring to a boil. Add the leeks and return to a boil. Boil leeks gently until tender, about 5 to 10 minutes, depending on age and diameter of leeks. Drain; set aside. Arrange the halibut steaks on a lightly greased shallow 2-quart casserole. Arrange leeks around halibut. Pour on the wine and fish bouillon. Bake for about 15 minutes, or until fish flakes easily with a fork. Remove fish and leeks to a serving platter. Cover with aluminum foil and keep warm. Strain wine liquid and reserve. In a small saucepan, heat the butter until melted. Add the shallots. Cook over medium heat until tender, about 3 to 5 minutes, stirring occasionally. Add wine liquid (about 1⅓ cups). Bring to a boil. Reduce over high heat to about ⅔ cup, about 8 to 10 minutes. Add the cream and return to a boil. Boil gently until slightly reduced, about 5 minutes. Stir in the lemon juice. Drain into sauce any juices that may have accumulated from fish. Season fish with salt and pepper to taste. Drizzle some sauce over fish. Garnish with the green onion. Pass the remaining sauce separately.

NOTE: You can, if you wish, use halibut steaks with bone (weight will be more, of course), but baking time may be slightly longer. Bake until fish flakes easily with a fork.

Scottish Herring Fried in Oatmeal

A basic recipe, to make in any desired quantity, this is a very Scottish dish, combining two staple foods of the country. Somehow the two flavors combine into an absolutely perfect food. Incidentally, oatmeal gives a delicious flavor to other fried fish when it is used as a coating instead of flour or crumbs.

Clean and bone the herring, and split in half. Season the oatmeal with salt and pepper to taste. Dip herring into oatmeal to coat on all sides, shaking off excess. Heat any fat (bacon fat is very good) to smoking point. Fry herring for 5 minutes on each side, or longer if large. Drain on paper towels and serve very hot with English Gooseberry Sauce, page 239.

ENGLISH KEDGEREE

This dish is said to be of Indian origin, prominent in Anglo-Indian cookery. Many recipes say that it can be made from any cooked white fish. It can, but the kedgeree will be rather flat. If, however, it is made from cooked smoked finnan haddock or filets of same, it is absolutely delicious. The smoky flavor of the fish blends particularly well with the rice and egg, and I urge all neophytes to try kedgeree at least once. Smoked finnan haddie is available at all good fish stores.

Serves 6

6 to 8 tablespoons butter
2 cups boiled rice
2 cups cooked flaked finnan haddie or other cooked white fish (see Note)
2 hard-boiled eggs, chopped
Salt
Freshly ground pepper
Chopped parsley

Heat the butter until golden but not brown. Add the rice, finnan haddie, and hard-boiled eggs, and season with salt and pepper to taste. Heat through over low heat; the dish must be very hot. Stir occasionally to prevent scorching. Serve very hot, garnished with parsley.

NOTE: To cook finnan haddie, poach in simmering water to cover. Cooking time depends on whether whole fish or fillet is used, as well as on the thickness of the fish. But cooking time is always short, and the fish should be flaky when cooked. Do not overcook; finnan haddie is already cooked to a certain extent by having been smoked. Drain; skin and bone before using.

Another way of making kedgeree is to separate the egg whites from the yolks. The whites are chopped and added to the rice and fish. The yolks are rubbed through a sieve and sprinkled on top of the kedgeree.

SALMON IN CHAMPAGNE

Serves 6

     6 salmon steaks (about 2½ to 3 pounds)
       Salt
       Freshly ground pepper
     ¼ cup butter, cut into pieces
    1½ cups champagne (good quality but not vintage)
     ½ cup heavy cream

Preheat the oven to slow (325° F).

   In a buttered baking dish, arrange the salmon steaks side by side. Sprinkle with salt and pepper to taste. Dot with the butter. Pour the champagne over the salmon. Bake according to thickness: 20 minutes for steaks 1 inch thick, 30 minutes for steaks 2 inches thick, or to 140° F on a meat thermometer. Baste the salmon frequently with the pan juices. When the salmon is just tender, transfer carefully to a warm serving dish. Cover with aluminum foil and keep warm. Pour the pan juices into a saucepan. Cook over high heat until reduced to about half. Stir in the cream. Simmer over low heat for about 3 minutes. Check the seasoning. Pour the sauce over the salmon and serve immediately.

BRAISED SALMON STEAKS IN WHITE WINE

Serves 6

 1 bouquet garni, made from:
 ¼ teaspoon dried thyme
 1 bay leaf
 2 sprigs parsley
 1 clove garlic, unpeeled
 2 tablespoons butter
 ½ cup minced shallots (6 large)
 6 salmon steaks, about ¾ to 1 inch thick (about 3⅓ pounds)
   About 2 cups dry white wine
 6 large egg yolks
 1½ cups heavy cream
   Salt
   Cayenne pepper

Preheat the oven to hot (400° F).

Make a bouquet garni: On a small piece of clean cheesecloth, place the thyme, bay leaf, parsley, and garlic. Bring sides of cheesecloth up around the herbs. Tie with string to enclose herbs and form a bundle; set aside.

Heat the butter in a small saucepan. Add the shallots and sauté over low heat for about 5 minutes, or until just tender, stirring occasionally. Do not brown. Spread the shallots evenly on bottom of a greased oblong 3-quart casserole. Top with the salmon steaks. Pour on the wine. The salmon should be barely covered; if necessary, add more wine. Add the bouquet garni. Bake for 15 to 20 minutes, or just until steaks flake easily with a fork. Remove salmon to a serving dish; cover with aluminum foil if necessary, or any fitting lid, and keep warm.

Strain wine mixture into a small saucepan and bring to a boil. Boil until reduced by one third or to about 1⅓ cups, about 8 minutes. In a bowl, beat well the egg yolks and cream. Add to reduced wine mixture. Whisk over low heat until mixture coats a metal spoon

(175° F on a candy thermometer). Season with salt and cayenne pepper to taste. Drain into sauce any juices that may have accumulated from fish. Spoon some of the sauce over salmon. Pour the remaining sauce into a warm serving bowl and serve with the fish.

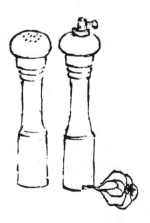

COQUILLES ST. JACQUES

Coquilles St. Jacques is an elegant scallop-and-cheese combination, and surprisingly easy to make. The scallop shells in which the scallops are baked can be bought in most fish or housewares stores. But there is no rule against baking them in a handsome ovenproof dish or in ovenproof ramekins.

Serves 4

1 pound fresh small scallops
Juice of 1 lemon
3 tablespoons butter
1 bay leaf
2 cups water
2 tablespoons flour
1 teaspoon salt
½ teaspoon ground white pepper
1 cup light cream
2 egg yolks
½ cup grated Swiss or Parmesan cheese
2 tablespoons dry white wine
Paprika

Preheat the oven to moderate (350° F).

Wash and dry the scallops. Sprinkle with the lemon juice. Simmer in water with 1 tablespoon of the butter, and the bay leaf for 5 minutes. Drain. Melt the remaining 2 tablespoons butter, and blend in the flour, salt, and pepper. Gradually stir in the cream, mixing until thick and smooth. Beat in the egg yolks and cheese. Cook for 3 minutes longer. Add the wine and scallops. Pour into buttered scallop shells and sprinkle with paprika. Bake for 10 to 15 minutes, or until top is golden brown.

NOTE: If you have large scallops only, cut them into pieces.

SCOTCH LOBSTER

The combination of lobster and Scotch whisky is an unexpected and very good one.

Serves 4

4 lobster tails, fresh or, if frozen, thawed (about 6 ounces each)
½ cup Scotch, warmed in a small saucepan
1 cup heavy cream
1 teaspoon soy or Worcestershire sauce
½ teaspoon salt
  Tabasco
1 tablespoon fresh lemon juice
¼ cup butter, at room temperature and cut into pieces

Drop the lobster tails into a large kettle of boiling salted water. Return to a boil and cook for 3 to 5 minutes, no longer. Drain and pour cold water over the tails. Drain again. With kitchen scissors, cut through the underside membrane of each tail. Remove the meat and slice. Put the lobster into a skillet. Sprinkle with the Scotch. Flame over medium heat. Shake the pan until the flames die down. Transfer the lobster pieces to a heated deep serving dish and keep warm. Add the cream, soy sauce, salt, and Tabasco to taste to the pan juices. Bring to a boil. Reduce the heat and return the lobster pieces to the skillet. Heat through and return lobster to heated serving dish. Stir the lemon juice and the butter into the pan juices and stir until melted. Check the seasoning and pour over the lobster. Serve very hot, with buttered rice.

LOBSTER CHARANTAIS

This dish may also be made with crabmeat.

Serves 4

¼ cup unsalted butter
6 green onions, white and green parts, sliced fine
½ sweet green pepper, minced
1 pound cooked lobster meat, cut into bite-size pieces
½ cup dry white wine
½ teaspoon dried tarragon
  Salt
  Freshly ground pepper
⅓ cup Cognac or brandy
1 tablespoon chopped parsley
  Toast triangles

Heat the butter in a skillet or a chafing dish. Add the green onions and pepper. Cook, stirring constantly, until the green onions are soft. Do not let them brown. Add the lobster meat, wine, and tarragon, and season with salt and pepper to taste. Cook over medium heat, stirring occasionally (stir carefully so as not to break the lobster pieces), for about 5 minutes, or until heated through thoroughly. Pour the Cognac into a large spoon or ladle and heat it quickly over direct heat. Pour over lobster meat and light. Let the flames die down. Sprinkle with the chopped parsley and serve spooned over toast triangles.

MOULES MARINIÈRES

The simplest of all mussel dishes and the most popular. Or use clams, if you prefer.

Serves 2

1 quart mussels or clams
2 teaspoons minced onion
2 teaspoons minced parsley
1 cup dry white wine
1 teaspoon salt
½ teaspoon freshly ground pepper

Scrub the mussels under cold running water and throw away any that are open. Combine all the ingredients in a large kettle. Cover tightly and cook over high heat for about 5 minutes, or until all the shells are open. Discard any mussels that remain closed. Drain mussels into a bowl and reserve the liquid. Put mussels into a deep dish and keep warm. Pour the mussel liquid into a small saucepan, leaving any sediment behind in the bowl. Over high heat, reduce the liquid by two thirds. Pour the sauce over the mussels and serve in soup plates with a soup spoon; have empty plates handy for the discarded shells.

NOTE: If a thicker sauce is wanted, knead together 1 tablespoon butter and 2 teaspoons flour. Stir into the reduced liquid and cook for 1 minute.

SHRIMPS IN CREAM

Serves 3 or 4

 1 pound cooked and shelled small shrimp, preferably deveined
 ½ cup Cognac or brandy
   Salt
   Freshly ground pepper
 ⅛ teaspoon dried marjoram
 6 tablespoons sweet butter
 ½ cup sherry, preferably dry
 4 egg yolks
 2 cups light or heavy cream
 ⅛ teaspoon ground nutmeg

Place the shrimp in a deep dish and sprinkle with the Cognac. Mix with a spoon to coat all the shrimp. Sprinkle with salt and pepper to taste, and add the marjoram. Mix again and let stand for 15 minutes. Heat the butter in a saucepan and add the shrimp. Cook, stirring frequently, for about 3 to 5 minutes over medium heat, or until the shrimp are pink and heated through thoroughly. Transfer the shrimp to a heated deep serving dish and keep warm. Stir the sherry into the pan juices. Over medium heat, stirring constantly, reduce the liquid by half. Beat together the egg yolks, cream, and nutmeg. Remove the pan from the heat and stir in the cream mixture. Return to very low heat and cook until hot and thickened. Do not let boil. Pour the sauce over the shrimp and serve with buttered rice.

VARIATION

Instead of shrimp, 2 chicken breasts, split, skin removed, and preferably boned can be used. But in this case, cook the chicken breasts in the butter about 8 minutes on either side, or until completely cooked. Proceed as above.

Spanish Shrimp (Salad)

ENSALADA DE CAMARONES

Serves 3 or 4

Dressing

 1 cup olive oil
 ¼ cup white wine vinegar or other white vinegar
 Juice of 1 large lemon
 Grated rind of ½ lemon
 1 clove garlic, minced
 2 to 3 tablespoons capers, drained
 1 teaspoon sugar
 ⅛ teaspoon Tabasco or other hot red pepper sauce
 Salt
 Freshly ground pepper
 2 to 3 cups cooked, shelled, and deveined shrimp
 1 large onion, thinly sliced
 Lettuce leaves
 Lemon and tomato slices

Combine all the dressing ingredients and blend thoroughly. Place the shrimp and onion slices in alternate layers in a deep bowl. Pour dressing over layers and chill at least 2 hours. To serve, drain off dressing. Place shrimp and onion on lettuce leaves and decorate with thin slices of lemon and tomato.

Court Bouillon with Dill for Poaching Fish

Here is an excellent court bouillon for poaching fish flavored with Sweden's favorite herb, dill.

About 1 quart

- 4 cups water
- ¼ cup white vinegar
- 1 tablespoon salt
- 3 whole allspice
- 1 bay leaf
- 1 small onion, chopped
- 1 3-inch piece carrot, chopped
- 5 to 10 sprigs fresh dill

Combine all the ingredients in a saucepan and bring to a boil. Cover and simmer for 15 to 20 minutes. Strain, and use liquid for poaching fish. Garnish cooked fish with additional dill sprigs or snipped dill.

NOTE: Poached fish is often served with a white sauce enriched with chopped hard-boiled eggs (½ egg for 1 cup sauce) and chopped dill.

A FINE CREAM SAUCE FOR ALL FISH

About 1 cup

⅔ cup heavy cream
⅓ cup A-1 Sauce
   Salt
   Freshly ground pepper
   Pinch sugar

Combine the cream and A-1 Sauce, and heat gently in the top of a double boiler over simmering, not boiling, water. The sauce must not boil. Season with a little salt and pepper, and add the sugar.

Chicken, a Few Other Birds, and One Rabbit Recipe

Since chicken is so far ahead of other birds in popularity, price, and abundance, this chapter is largely dedicated to it. The number of ways of cooking chicken is indeed legion, perhaps because this most domesticated of all birds has the great advantage of producing edible flesh cheaply and with far less trouble than any other animal. Chickens will fend for themselves if not fed, and though the meat of such free-ranging fowl may be tough, it is certainly edible and much more flavorful.

In this context I remember the chickens in the country around Seville, where I once lived in an orange grove—never mind why. They were fierce and determined birds with more than one strain of fighting cock in them, derived from their mothers mating with the survivors of the time-honored local sport of cock fighting. Since the barren soil of their yard was most unrewarding, these enterprising fowl lived in the orange groves and supported themselves on orange windfalls and the oranges that we threw away by the dozens after sucking them. These Spanish chickens were not afraid of man or dog, and had to be chased away with a stick. When they came to the table, everyone felt a sense of personal triumph, seeing the enemy down at last. They tasted uniquely and wonderfully of orange, and the toughness of their athletic bodies mattered no longer, since they had been stewed gently and long in fragrant, spur-of-the-moment casseroles made with tenderizing white or red wine, tomatoes, and whatever vegetables were at hand, with a pinch of coriander, cinnamon, or saffron thrown in, depending on the whim of the cook.

Those Spanish chickens may have been tough, but those birds had plenty of flavor, whereas our mass-produced chickens are the consistency of tender flannel and have no flavor of their own. Besides their cheapness, low caloric content, and easy availability, this lack of flavor may be one of the reasons people today like chicken so much. Like pasta, it is a neutral food and you can do anything you want with it. Since chicken is now a common food, my ideas on the different ways of cooking the birds follow.

COOKING METHODS

ROASTING. I do not intend to get in on the great controversy as to whether chickens should be roasted at high heat, with constant basting, or at medium heat. Personally, I roast birds up to 3 pounds in weight in a 400° to 425° F oven, and larger chickens in a moderate (350° F) oven, with excellent results. Again, and this is my own opinion, I think that a small bird dries out if cooked at the lower temperature. Agreed that poultry, like other meats, is only truly roasted if cooked on a spit in circulating dry air—and incomparably better that way than if prepared in any other way—I leave it to the cook to roast a chicken in the way that has given the best results. But I do think that in oven-roasting, the birds should first be sprinkled with salt and pepper both inside and out, and rubbed with soft butter or with a mixture of butter and olive oil. Bigger birds ought to have a piece of larding pork or bacon tied onto their breasts to prevent the breast from browning too quickly and from drying out while the slower-cooking legs finish roasting. The chicken should be placed on a rack, so that it will be roasted all around, rather than roasted on top and steamed in its own juices underneath, which will happen if it is allowed to lie in the pan juices.

I am also a great believer in constant basting, and here I agree with French chefs that only fat—especially butter—should be used for basting a roasting chicken. Some authorities claim that butter mixed with chicken broth or hot water makes for a more succulent gravy, and I dare say they are right if you are interested in gravy. But as for the chicken, I say baste it with melted butter that is kept hot on the stove. Pan juices for basting are apt to deposit the little burned bits on the chicken, which are delicious in the gravy but not on the chicken's complexion.

And don't forget to turn the chicken during the roasting process so that the underside will be done as perfectly as the breast side.

CASSEROLED CHICKEN. Chicken casseroles can be made up on the spur of the moment with whatever vegetables, herbs, and seasonings are available. The beginning is always the same: the fowl, either whole or cut in pieces, is sautéed in fat until golden on all sides. The fat can be butter, bacon, lard, salt pork, or olive oil, depending on the flavor the finished dish is to have and the ingredients that will be cooked with the chicken. Heavy vegetables, such as turnips, carrots, potatoes, etc., benefit from the fat of the pig. Delicate vegetables, such as peas, young string beans, and artichoke hearts, are better off with a butter beginning. Perfectionists differentiate between the vegetables used to season the casserole (onions, carrots, and celery, for instance) and the vegetables that are to be eaten. They say the first vegetables should be strained out of the sauce when the fowl is cooked three fourths of the way, and the eating vegetables should be added after having been browned in a little butter. I agree with this point of view.

The liquid for a classic chicken casserole is hot chicken bouillon, wine, sometimes tomato juice or apple cider, and even the chicken's blood in many French recipes. Or there are mixtures of these liquids. Excessive fat is poured out after browning the bird and is to be skimmed from the sauce before serving the chicken. This is not easy, and in my experience it is better to use no more than the barest amount of fat needed to brown the bird in order to make this degreasing process easier.

Often, sweet or sour cream and egg yolks beaten together are added to a casserole to thicken and flavor the sauce. The prevailing practice is to add the cream to the finished dish and let it heat through without boiling, to avoid curdling the sauce. But in some casseroles the chicken is cooked, or rather simmered, in the cream alone. This makes for a tastier though less attractive dish.

SKINNING, TRIMMING, ETC. Experts disagree as to whether birds other than roasters should be skinned before cooking. I skin and trim away every bit of skin, fat, tendons, and superfluous matter before cooking any chicken other than a roaster.

Then, I heat the chicken, now a naked piece of meat. Since chicken is inexpensive nowadays and can also be bought in parts, I never use the wings and backs of a cut-up chicken for anything but making bouillon. Why penalize people with the lesser parts of the bird when it costs but little more to make a casserole of legs and breasts, if not breasts alone?

A cook's good common sense should prevail when it comes to the cooking time of chickens and their sauces. The cooking time in the following recipes is as nearly correct as I can make it. But most chicken dishes can be done with any kind of fowl, and furthermore, any bird's tenderness varies with its age, so that the cook has to test for doneness. American chickens are very tender, and the cooking time of European recipes is often much too long for our fowl. Chickens should not be overdone, but they should be well done, and cooked through thoroughly and completely.

The cook has also to rely on her judgment when it comes to the consistency of the sauce. If it is too thin, it can be either boiled down after the chicken is ready and kept hot on a separate plate, or else the dish can be cooked without a cover. The sauce can also be thickened with *beurre manié*: equal parts of butter and flour (or two parts butter to one part flour, depending on how rich the sauce is to be) kneaded together into small, pea-sized balls, which are stirred one after the other into the sauce until the right consistency is reached.

A sauce that is too thick can be thinned with a little more wine, bouillon or water—all added very hot, a tablespoon at a time, until the right consistency has been achieved.

As a final word of encouragement, I should like to say that ingredients for casseroles made with fowl, like all casseroles, do not have to be measured with the utmost accuracy, as must those for a cake. Let expediency and one's own taste triumph in this case.

The number of servings to be derived from a chicken is a moot point. When buying a roasting chicken, allow 1 pound for each person. But when the chicken is cut up, the cook will have to decide on the number of servings. A 2½- to 3-pound chicken can serve four if every bit is utilized and if the eaters are served small portions. If only legs and breasts are used, it is for the cook to decide whether each guest is to have one or two pieces. All I can describe in the following recipes is how to cook a chicken of a certain size, and leave it to the cook to double the recipe if necessary.

It is taken for granted that the chicken is truly ready to cook—that is, properly cleaned and plucked, washed and dried—and that it will be served on a good-size plate so that the bird does not slither around as you cut it, and fall on the table.

QUICK AND SIMPLE SKILLET CHICKEN

The wine makes all the difference.
Low in calories, too.

Serves 3

1 3-pound chicken, cut into serving pieces
  Salt
  Freshly ground pepper
3 tablespoons olive oil
1 tablespoon butter
1 to 2 tablespoons dried rosemary, crumbled
2 whole cloves garlic
½ cup dry white wine

Trim the fat from the chicken pieces, and if you like, remove the skin as well. Rub chicken with salt and pepper. Heat the olive oil and butter in a large skillet. Brown chicken pieces on all sides. Sprinkle chicken with the rosemary. Add the garlic and wine. Bring to a boil, then reduce the heat to low. Simmer, covered, for about 15 to 20 minutes, or until chicken is tender. Add a little more wine if necessary, to prevent drying out, but add only a few tablespoons at a time since this is not a saucy dish. Serve with a green vegetable.

CHICKEN WITH CURRIED CREAM SAUCE

This is a French dish. French cooks like to use curry powder to flavor a sauce lightly, although they don't like to make dishes spicy with it as the Indians and Americans do.

Serves 4 to 6

1 3- to 4-pound chicken, cut into 8 pieces (do not use backs)
3 tablespoons butter
1 medium onion, minced
1 cup hot chicken bouillon
¼ cup Cognac or brandy
1½ cups heavy cream
1 to 2 teaspoons curry powder
   Salt
   Freshly ground pepper
1 teaspoon butter kneaded with 1 teaspoon flour
2 tablespoons minced parsley

Trim the fat from the chicken pieces, and if you like, remove the skin as well. Heat the butter in a large deep skillet. Brown chicken pieces over medium heat. Add the onion and chicken bouillon. Reduce the heat to low and simmer, covered, for about 30 minutes, or until chicken is tender. Raise the heat to medium; heat the Cognac in a small saucepan and pour it over chicken. Flame, shaking the pan so that chicken pieces flame evenly. Transfer chicken to a heated serving dish and keep warm.

Skim off all the fat from the pan juices. Reduce the heat to low and stir in the cream and curry powder. Simmer the sauce for about 5 to 6 minutes, stirring occasionally. Check the seasoning; add salt and pepper to taste. Stir the butter and flour mixture into the sauce and cook for 1 minute longer. Pour the sauce over chicken pieces and sprinkle with the parsley. Serve with asparagus, broccoli, or another green vegetable.

BRAISED CHICKEN NANTAISE

A classic French dish.

Serves 4

1 bouquet garni, made from:
¼ teaspoon dried thyme
1 bay leaf
3 sprigs parsley
1 clove garlic
3 tablespoons butter
1 4-pound chicken, quartered
1 teaspoon paprika
  Salt
  Freshly ground pepper
⅓ cup dry white wine
½ teaspoon white vinegar
¼ pound small whole white onions, peeled, trimmed, and cooked in boiling water until almost tender, 10 to 15 minutes, and well drained
½ pound small mushrooms with stems, stems trimmed, or medium to large mushrooms, quartered or cut into eights
2 tablespoons tomato paste
¼ cup heavy cream
1 teaspoon cornstarch mixed with 1 tablespoon water and blended until smooth
  Minced parsley (optional)

Make a bouquet garni: On a small piece of clean cheesecloth, place the thyme, bay leaf, parsley, and garlic. Bring sides of cheesecloth up around the herbs. Tie with string to enclose herbs and form a bundle; set aside.

Heat the butter in a heavy Dutch oven. Brown the chicken pieces over medium to medium-high heat for about 10 minutes, turning once. Sprinkle chicken with the paprika, ½ teaspoon salt, and ¼ teaspoon pepper. Pour in the wine. Add the vinegar and bouquet garni.

Bring to a boil, then reduce the heat to low. Cover and simmer for about 20 to 25 minutes, or until chicken is tender, turning occasionally. Remove chicken to a heated serving platter and keep warm.

Add the onions and mushrooms to cooking liquid. Bring to a boil, then reduce the heat to low. Cook, uncovered, until mushrooms and onions are tender, about 5 to 10 minutes. Stir in the tomato paste, cream, and cornstarch mixture. Simmer until sauce is hot and slightly thickened. Check the seasoning; add salt and pepper if necessary. Pour sauce over chicken. Garnish with parsley if desired. Serve with buttered boiled potatoes, preferably new ones, and a tossed salad.

STUFFED NORMANDY CHICKEN

A famous French recipe. A good Calvados is essential for the flavor of the dish.

Serves 5 or 6

1 4- to 5-pound roasting chicken
2 tablespoons butter
1 cup soft white bread crumbs
2 cups peeled, cored, and chopped tart apple
⅛ teaspoon ground cinnamon
  Salt
  Freshly ground pepper
2 to 4 tablespoons dry white wine or dry vermouth
  Butter, softened
½ cup chicken bouillon
⅔ cup Calvados
1 to 1½ cups heavy cream

Remove all visible fat from the chicken. Wipe inside with a damp cloth. Heat the butter in a skillet. Cook the bread crumbs until golden. Add the apple and cinnamon, and season with salt and pepper to taste. Mix well. Cook over medium heat, stirring constantly, until apple begins to soften. Stir in just enough wine to hold mixture together. Cool.

Preheat the oven to moderate (350° F). Stuff the chicken with the cooled apple mixture. Truss chicken; that is, fasten the wings and legs to the body with kitchen string. Rub chicken generously with the softened butter. Place on a rack in a shallow roasting pan, laying it on its side. Pour the bouillon and ¼ cup of the Calvados into the pan. Roast for 30 minutes, basting frequently with the pan juices. Turn chicken to other side and roast 30 minutes, basting frequently. Turn chicken on its back, breast side up, and roast 30 more minutes, basting frequently. The chicken should be golden, and the juices of the leg joint, when pricked with a skewer, should run clear. Transfer chicken to a heated serving platter and cut off the trussing strings. Turn off the heat and put chicken back into the oven to keep warm. Skim off all the fat from the pan juices. Scrape up all the brown bits at the bottom. Put pan on stove over lowest possible heat. Stir in the remaining Calvados and the cream. Heat through thoroughly, but do not let boil. Carve the chicken and pour the sauce over it or pass separately in a sauce boat. Serve with buttered rice and a *nonsweet*, thick, hot applesauce.

MANGO CHICKEN

A mildly exotic dish that will not frighten those who do not like exotic food. Apricots or papaya may be used instead of mango, but mango is best.

Serves 4

1 4-pound roasting chicken, quartered
2 tablespoons butter
2 tablespoons salad oil
2 large or 4 medium onions, thinly sliced
1 to 2 mangoes, depending on size, peeled and chopped (about 2 to 3 cups pulp), or 2 cups pitted, mashed apricots or 1 cup dried apricots, plumped in lukewarm water for 1 hour, and drained, or 2 to 3 cups mashed papaya
¼ cup mango chutney
⅔ cup chicken bouillon or water
    Salt
    Freshly ground pepper
⅛ teaspoon ground nutmeg
    Rind of 1 lime, green part only, shredded fine
    Juice of 1 lime

Preheat the oven to moderate (350° F).

Remove all visible fat from the chicken. Cut off the wing tips and remove the skin. Wash and pat dry. Heat the butter and salad oil in a large frying pan. Sauté the chicken pieces until golden brown on all sides. Transfer chicken to a heavy 3-quart casserole. Add the onions to the skillet and cook over low heat, stirring frequently, until very soft but still white. Add the mangoes and the mango chutney. Raise the heat to medium and cook the mixture for 3 more minutes, stirring constantly. Stir in the chicken bouillon. Season with salt and pepper to taste, and stir in the nutmeg. Pour the mixture over chicken. Add the lime rind. Cover and bake for about 45 minutes to 1 hour, or until chicken is cooked. Stir in the lime juice. Serve as is or, better yet, clear the chicken pieces of the fruit and onions, and transfer them to a heated serving platter and keep warm. Purée the fruit, onions, and cooking liquid in a blender and pour over the chicken pieces. If the sauce gets cold doing this, heat it up, but do not let boil. Serve with pilaff and a green vegetable.

NOTE: You may have to adjust the consistency of the sauce. If it looks too thick and is in danger of scorching, add a little more bouillon or water.

CHICKEN MARENGO

I don't use the wings, backs, trimmings, necks, and gizzard for this dish, but use them to make bouillon. I make the bouquet garni with 2 bay leaves, 1 teaspoon dried thyme, and 4 parsley sprigs tied in a piece of cheesecloth. If I don't have any cheesecloth, I tie the bay leaves and parsley together with thread so that they can be removed later, and just sprinkle the thyme into the pot. Using shallots makes a world of difference to the dish.

Serves 5 or 6

- 1 pound medium mushrooms
- 2 2½- to 3-pound chickens, cut into 8 pieces each
- ¼ cup olive oil
- ⅔ cup minced shallots
- 1 bouquet garni (see page 126)
- ⅓ cup dry white wine
- ⅓ cup dry Madeira
- 1 large ripe tomato, peeled, seeded, and chopped, or 1 to 2 table-spoons tomato paste, dissolved in 2 tablespoons hot water
  Salt
  Freshly ground pepper
- 2 tablespoons butter
- 1 tablespoon lemon juice

Chop the stems off the mushrooms and reserve for other use. Drop the mushroom caps into a bowl filled with cold water and wash them by swishing them around with both hands (mushrooms grow in dirt). Do this very quickly or the mushrooms will become waterlogged. To dry the mushrooms, blot them thoroughly with paper towels.

Cut off wings and backs from chicken and reserve for soup. Skin the chicken pieces and remove all visible fat. Heat the olive oil in a deep frying pan large enough to take all the ingredients (12 inches or more) or in a sautoir of the same size. Add the chicken pieces, the shallots, and the bouquet garni. Cook over medium-low heat for about 10 to 12 minutes, or until pieces are golden brown. Turn to cook on all sides; use two wooden spoons to do this so as not to bruise or pierce the chicken. Add the mushrooms, wine, Madeira, and tomato, mixing with the wooden spoons. Cover and cook over medium heat for 10 minutes. Remove the cover and cook for 5 more minutes. In a low oven, heat a deep serving dish while the chicken is cooking. Test for doneness: the juices of the leg joint, when pricked with a skewer, should run clear; if not, cook for 5 minutes longer. Remove the bouquet garni. Transfer the chicken pieces neatly to the heated serving dish. Season with salt and pepper to taste. Add the butter to the pan and stir to thicken the sauce. Stir in the lemon juice. Pour sauce and mushrooms over the chicken and serve hot, with buttered rice or pilaff.

NOTE: Since mushrooms and tomatoes yield different amounts of liquid, the sauce may be too thin. In this case, mix 1 tablespoon of the butter with 1 or 2 teaspoons flour and stir into the sauce. Cook, stirring, for 1 minute, and then stir in the remaining tablespoon butter and the lemon juice.

FRENCH MINCED CHICKEN À LA RITZ

The following recipe came from the late, extremely lamented, and never equaled Ritz Hotel in New York, whose cooking was world-famous thanks to the late Louis Diat, a great, great chef and one of the nicest men who ever lived.

Serves 3

4 chicken breasts
Chicken bouillon
2 tablespoons butter
1 cup sliced mushrooms
½ cup minced sweet green pepper
¼ cup minced pimiento
⅔ cup dry sherry
1 cup heavy cream
1½ to 2 cups rich white or bechamel sauce (from a standard recipe)
1 teaspoon salt

Simmer the chicken breasts in chicken bouillon to cover until tender. Skin and bone, removing any fat and tendons. Mince fine. (You may also use 3 to 4 cups of the white meat of leftover chicken for this dish.) Heat the butter in a heavy skillet until golden, not brown, and sauté the mushrooms, pepper, and pimiento for about 5 minutes. Add the chicken, ⅓ cup of the sherry, and the cream. Simmer over low heat for about 10 minutes, or until the sauce is reduced by half. (It is not necessary to be deadly accurate about this; the purpose of this step is to have the chicken absorb most of the sherry and cream.) Add the white sauce and blend thoroughly. Season with the salt. Just before serving, stir in the remaining ⅓ cup sherry and a little more heavy cream if the sauce looks too thick. Serve with white or wild rice, or on buttered toast.

STEWED PORTUGUESE CHICKEN

Serves 4

1 4-pound roasting chicken, cut in 4 pieces
  Flour
  Salt
  Freshly ground pepper
¾ cup olive oil
2 cloves garlic, minced
1 medium onion, chopped
2 cups dry white wine
  Hot chicken bouillon
1 bay leaf
⅛ teaspoon dried thyme
1 teaspoon saffron, powdered or in threads
15 blanched almonds, finely chopped
½ cup coarse bread crumbs
  Olive oil for frying crumbs
2 hard-boiled eggs, chopped
¼ cup chopped parsley

Remove all visible fat from the chicken pieces. With a sharp knife, cut backbones away from breast pieces and trim off wing tips; reserve for soup. Coat chicken pieces in flour that has been seasoned with salt and pepper. Shake off excess flour. Heat the olive oil in a heavy skillet. Add the garlic and onion, and cook for about 5 minutes, or until soft. Add chicken and cook over medium heat until just golden; pieces should not be brown. Add the wine and enough chicken bouillon to barely cover chicken. Check the seasoning and add salt and pepper if needed. Add the bay leaf and thyme. Cover and simmer over low heat for about 30 minutes, or until chicken is almost tender.

Dissolve the saffron in a little hot water. When chicken is tender, add dissolved saffron and the almonds. Simmer for about 15 minutes longer, or until chicken is tender. If the sauce looks too thin, cook uncovered to allow for evaporation.

Fry the bread crumbs in a little olive oil until crisp and brown. Before serving, sprinkle chicken with the hard-boiled eggs, bread crumbs, and parsley. Serve with boiled new potatoes and a hot green vegetable salad.

POULET À LA CRÈME

Be sure to remove all visible fat from the chicken and get out as much fat as possible from under the skin.

Serves 4

1	3- to 3½-pound chicken
	Salt
	Freshly ground pepper
½	lemon, sliced
2	tablespoons butter
1	tablespoon oil
3	medium onions, finely chopped
½	pound mushrooms, sliced
½	cup dry white wine or water
1	teaspoon flour
½	cup heavy cream
	Dash ground nutmeg
2	tablespoons Cognac or brandy

Remove all visible fat from the chicken, and season the cavity with salt and pepper. Put the lemon slices into cavity. Truss the chicken; that is, fasten the wings and legs to the body with kitchen string. Heat the butter and oil in a flameproof casserole large enough to hold the chicken and vegetables; do not choose too large a casserole. Add the chicken. Cook it over medium to low heat, turning it several times, until browned on all sides. This will take about 5 to 10 minutes. Pour out all but about 2 tablespoons of fat from the casserole. Check the seasoning and add the onions. Cook, stirring the onions frequently, until they are golden brown. Add the mushrooms and wine. Cover the casserole and cook the chicken over medium heat for about 35 minutes. Test for doneness by pricking with a fork; the juices that run out should be clear. If still reddish, cook for 5 to 10 minutes longer.

Transfer chicken to a heated platter and keep warm in a low oven. Skim off any visible fat from the pan juices, then blot with paper towels to remove remaining fat. Stir the flour into the cream until smooth and stir mixture into pan juices. Bring to a boil and remove from heat. Check the seasoning, and if necessary, add more salt and pepper. Stir in the nutmeg. Leave the sauce as is, or, as I prefer it, whirl it in a food processor or blender. Stir in the Cognac and return sauce to low heat to keep hot. It should be very hot but not boiling. Remove trussing strings from chicken and either carve it in the kitchen, placing the pieces on a heated platter and drizzling a few tablespoons of sauce over the pieces to keep them moist, or place the whole chicken on a heated platter and carve it at the table. Turn sauce into a bowl and pass it separately. Serve with mashed potatoes or plain rice and a green salad.

NOTE: If you find it too difficult to pour off the excess fat from the casserole with the chicken in it, heat the butter and oil in a large frying pan. Brown the chicken on all sides and transfer the bird to a casserole. Add the onions to the fat in the frying pan and cook, stirring frequently, until golden brown. Use a slotted spoon to transfer the onions to the chicken in the casserole, and add 2 tablespoons of the fat in the frying pan to the casserole. Add the mushrooms and wine, and proceed as above.

Any leftover sauce can be used to dress noodles.

SWISS BAKED CHICKEN

The trick of the dish is to use fresh coarse bread crumbs, or rather shreds of fresh white bread, and plenty of sweet butter. The best way of making these coarse crumbs is to trim the crusts from the bread and pull the slices apart with your fingers.

Serves 2 to 4

1 2½- to 3-pound chicken, cut in serving pieces
  Salt
  Ground white pepper
1 cup sweet butter (or more)
½ loaf fresh white bread, shredded into coarse crumbs

Preheat the oven to moderate (350° F).

Skin and trim the chicken pieces. Sprinkle with salt and pepper to taste. Cream the butter until very soft. Spread each chicken piece thinly with butter. Place chicken in a buttered baking dish. Scatter the bread crumbs evenly over chicken. Dot with more butter. Bake for 30 to 40 minutes, or until chicken is tender and crumbs are golden and crisp. Serve from baking dish. A fairly tart salad—watercress, for instance—goes well with this dish. Or a salad of hot broccoli or string beans dressed with a vinaigrette dressing. No potatoes, rice, or noodles are needed, since the bread takes their place.

CHICKEN TOURANGELLE WITH MUSHROOMS AND ONIONS

Delicious—inspired by the French magazine Elle.

Serves 6

6 tablespoons butter
2 2½- to 2¾-pound chickens, each cut into quarters
¼ cup minced shallots
⅓ cup brandy
3 cups dry white wine
2 teaspoons salt, or to taste
2 teapoons dried tarragon
½ teaspoon freshly ground pepper
2 medium cloves garlic, crushed
2 large egg yolks
½ cup heavy cream
½ teaspoon fresh lemon juice
¾ pound small white onions, peeled, trimmed, and cooked in boiling water until tender, about 10 to 15 minutes, and well drained
¾ pound mushrooms, sliced
  Freshly ground pepper
  Minced parsley

Heat 2 tablespoons of the butter in a large, heavy Dutch oven. Add 1 quartered chicken and lightly brown over medium to medium-high heat for about 10 minutes, turning once. Remove chicken and set aside. Lightly brown the remaining chicken in the pan drippings. Remove chicken and set aside. Add the shallots to pan drippings. Cook over medium-high heat until tender, about 2 to 3 minutes. Return chicken to Dutch oven. Pour on the brandy and heat briefly over low heat. Shielding your face, ignite the brandy with a lighted match. Shake Dutch oven back and forth for several seconds until flames subside. Pour in the wine. Add the salt, tarragon, and pepper.

Bring to a boil, then reduce the heat to low. Simmer, covered, until chicken is tender, about 30 minutes, turning pieces occasionally. Remove chicken to a heated deep serving platter and keep warm. Add the garlic to wine mixture. Bring to a boil and boil gently until mixture is reduced almost by half (2 to 2⅓ cups). Reduce the heat to low. Blend the egg yolks and heavy cream until smooth. Stir into the wine mixture. Heat over low heat until hot. Stir in the lemon juice. Check the seasoning and add more salt if necessary. Remove to a small saucepan; simmer to keep warm, but do not let boil. Heat the remaining 4 tablespoons butter in a Dutch oven. Add the mushrooms and onions. Cook over medium-high heat just until tender, 3 to 5 minutes; do not overcook. Season with salt and pepper to taste. Pour sauce over chicken. Garnish with parsley. Serve with a buttered green vegetable such as zucchini.

CHINESE WALNUT CHICKEN

Serves 4 to 6

    3 chicken breasts, cut in half
    1 cup shelled walnuts
    ¼ cup salad oil
    ½ cup sliced green onions, white and green parts
    1 tablespoon cornstarch
    ¼ to ½ teaspoon ground ginger
    ¼ cup water
    ¼ cup dry or medium sweet sherry
    2 tablespoons soy sauce

Remove the skin and any visible fat from the chicken breasts. Cut the meat from the breasts, cutting it as nearly as possible into 1-inch squares. Blanch the walnuts; that is, cover them with cold water, bring to a boil, and simmer for 3 minutes. Drain, rinse with cold water, and rub off the skins with both hands. Heat the oil in a skillet. Add the walnuts. Cook, stirring constantly, until the walnuts are golden. Remove them with a slotted spoon to a piece of paper towel. Add the chicken and the green onions. Cook for 5 minutes over high heat, stirring constantly. Blend together the cornstarch, ginger, water, sherry, and soy sauce to make a smooth paste. Stir into the chicken mixture. Reduce the heat. Cover and simmer for about 5 minutes, or until the sauce is thickened and the chicken tender. Stir frequently. Stir in the walnuts. Serve hot over plain rice.

COLD CHICKEN WITH TUNA SAUCE

A variation on the famous Italian summer dish, vitello tonnato, *based on an inexpensive meat and almost as good.*

Serves 4 to 6

  4 large chicken breasts, cut in half, and skinned and boned
1½ cups dry white wine
  1 medium onion, thinly sliced
  1 clove garlic, mashed
  1 7-ounce can tuna, drained and flaked
  6 anchovy fillets, drained and cut into pieces
 ¼ teaspoon salt
   Freshly ground pepper
  1 tablespoon grated lemon rind
 ¼ cup olive oil
  3 tablespoons fresh lemon juice
  2 tablespoons capers, drained (optional)
   Tomato wedges

Put the chicken breasts into a heavy casserole. Add the wine, onion, garlic, tuna, anchovy fillets, salt, pepper, and lemon rind. Bring to a boil, reduce the heat immediately, and simmer, covered, for about 25 minutes, or until the chicken is cooked. Check occasionally, and if too dry, add a little more wine. Transfer the chicken to a deep serving dish that can go to the table. Cool. Purée the rest of the contents of the casserole in a blender, and stir in the olive oil and lemon juice. Mix well. Sauce should have the consistency of a thick pancake batter. Pour the sauce evenly over the chicken. Sprinkle with the capers. Cover with plastic wrap and refrigerate for 8 hours or overnight. Decorate the dish with tomato wedges, and serve with a tossed green salad and Italian bread.

CHICKEN LIVERS WITH SAGE

Chicken livers and fresh sage are a great flavor combination typical of Tuscany and Rome. Dried sage can be used in a pinch, but it is worthwhile to take the trouble to find fresh sage for this dish.

Serves 3

   1 pound chicken livers, trimmed
     Salt
     Freshly ground pepper
  12 chopped fresh sage leaves or 1 tablespoon dried sage
  ¼ cup butter
   2 slices bacon, diced
  ¼ cup dry white wine

Cut the chicken livers in half if they are large. Season with salt and pepper to taste, and coat with the sage. Heat the butter and bacon together in a skillet. Sauté livers for 5 to 6 minutes. Add the white wine and simmer for 2 minutes longer. Serve as is for a first course, or with a vegetable salad as a main dish.

DUCKLING WITH OLIVES

Serves 4

1 5- to 6-pound duckling
2 cups drained pimiento-stuffed olives
2 tablespoons flour
1 cup Madeira
¼ teaspoon freshly ground pepper
½ teaspoon dried thyme
3 sprigs parsley
1 stalk celery
2 bay leaves

Preheat the oven to hot (425° F).

Remove any visible fat from the duckling. Stuff duckling with 1 cup of the olives. Truss duckling; that is, fasten the wings and legs close to the body with kitchen string. Prick duckling all over with a fork. Place on a rack in a shallow roasting pan. Roast duckling for 10 minutes. Reduce the oven temperature to moderate (350° F) and roast for 20 minutes longer. Transfer duckling to a heated serving platter and keep warm.

Pour off all the fat in the pan except for 1 tablespoon. Scrape up all the brown bits at the bottom of the pan. Stir the flour into the pan drippings and cook over low heat for 1 minute. Stir in the Madeira and cook, stirring constantly, until the sauce is thick and smooth. Add the pepper, thyme, parsley, celery, and bay leaves. Return duckling to the pan. Cover the pan and roast duckling in the same moderate (350° F) oven for about 45 minutes. Transfer the duckling to the heated platter and keep warm. Remove the parsley, celery, and bay leaves from the sauce. Stir in the remaining 1 cup olives and heat through quickly. Pour the sauce over the duckling and serve immediately, with creamed potatoes.

HASENPFEFFER

Germans make this with hare, which has a sharper flavor than rabbit.

Serves 4 to 6

¼ pound salt pork or bacon, diced small
⅓ cup butter
3 large onions, thinly sliced
1 3- to 4-pound rabbit, fresh or frozen (thawed), cut into serving pieces
3 bay leaves, crumbled
1½ cups full-bodied dry red wine
2 tablespoons wine vinegar
1 cup water
1 tablespoon sugar
Salt
Freshly ground pepper
2 tablespoons cornstarch mixed with ¼ cup water and blended until smooth

Pour boiling water over the salt pork or bacon and let stand for 3 minutes. Drain. Heat half the butter in a skillet with the pork. Cook until crisp, but do not let brown. Add the onions. Cook, stirring constantly, until onions are soft and golden. Heat the remaining butter in a large casserole and brown the rabbit pieces on all sides. Add the salt pork, onions, and pan juices to the rabbit. Add the bay leaves, wine, vinegar, water, and sugar. Season with salt and pepper to taste. Cover tightly and simmer for about 40 minutes longer, or until tender (cooking time depends on the age of the rabbit).

Transfer the rabbit pieces to a heated serving dish and keep warm. Skim off the fat from the pan juices. Cook over high heat, scraping up the brown bits at the bottom, until reduced to 1½ cups. Stir the cornstarch mixture into the sauce. Cook, stirring constantly, until smooth and thickened. Spoon the sauce over the rabbit pieces and serve with home-fried potatoes and a tossed green salad.

NOTE: If desired, stir ¼ cup heavy cream into the sauce. In this case, thicken it with only 1 tablespoon cornstarch and 2 tablespoons water.

QUAIL WITH ORANGE SAUERKRAUT

The recipe, or rather cooking method, is for small birds—
1 per serving. You have to adjust cooking time to age and
size of birds . . . and know something about cooking.

Quail (1 per person)
½ lemon
Juniper berries
Salt pork or bacon slices
Butter, melted
Brandy
Heavy cream (about ¼ cup per bird)
Oranges
Butter
Sauerkraut
Salt
Freshly ground pepper
Orange slices and parsley sprigs or watercress

Preheat the oven to hot (400° F).

Wash the quail thoroughly and dry. Rub cavity and skin with lemon. Put 2 juniper berries into cavity of each bird. Wrap salt pork or bacon slices around the breasts, and tie with kitchen string. Truss the birds or push legs towards the breast and fasten with a skewer pushed through both legs and the middle of the bird. Roast for 15 minutes in a roasting pan, basting frequently. Five minutes before the birds are done, raise the heat to hot (450° F) and remove salt pork or bacon slices. Brown breasts thoroughly. Flame brandy by lighting it in a warmed ladle. Pour over birds. Remove birds to a heated platter and keep warm. Stir the cream into pan juices and simmer over moderate heat for 3 to 4 minutes. Pour over birds.

For each quart of sauerkraut, use 1 large orange. Peel and remove all white membrane. Cut orange into 1-inch pieces. Cook in hot butter (¼ cup per orange) for 3 to 4 minutes. Drain the sauerkraut and add to orange. Season with salt and pepper to taste. Cover and simmer for 10 minutes. Drain.

Serve each bird on a mound of rather stiff, buttery mashed potatoes. Surround with sauerkraut. Decorate platter with thin orange slices and parsley or watercress sprigs.

Meats

The plaintive cries of returning travelers complaining that they "can't understand why things taste so much better in Europe than when I cook them" usually indicate confusion over methods of preparation and lack of knowledge of what's suitable for what. The various terms and methods used in meat cookery seem to be in a particular muddle.

The cooking of meats is a vast, noble, and controversial subject—at least in its finer points. Much has been written about it by great and small American, European, and Chinese masters, often in acrimonious tones. Nevertheless, there are a number of common principles. The first of these is that the meat must be suited to the purpose to which it will be put, and the second, that the correct method of cooking must be used.

Since any good standard cookbook tells the proper use for every kind of meat, there is no need to repeat this information here. But it is well to bear in mind that in these days of the vanishing butcher, when most meat is cut behind the scenes by invisible and unskillful gnomes armed with hacksaws instead of good butcher knives, it is extremely important to trim one's own meat. A good butcher will do it, but most butchers are not good and they are also conscious of their advantage: fat is cheap and meat is not, you pay for the latter while getting much of the former. You can't forever fight your butcher, but you can at least get what meat you have into the shape you want it by trimming it yourself. Now, a few basic rules to be observed in meat cookery.

ROASTING. Roasted meats should be cooked so they are full of their own juices, sealed within. Red meats should have rosy—not bloody—juices; white meats, white—never pinkish—juices. There is but one true roasting process: the spit turning over an open fire, or its nearest modern equivalent, the electric rotisserie. Both allow the fundamental principle of roasting to take place: namely, to let dry air circulate freely around the meat while it cooks. The taste and succulence of genuinely roasted meats cannot be reproduced by any other process.

Oven roasting, even in a low, open pan as it should be done, in my opinion, is really a baking process. Fresh, dry air cannot circulate freely in an oven and some steam will accumulate. But as oven roasting is the method we must use in daily cooking, let us observe a few rules for best results. In order to let as much air as possible flow around the meat, it should always be set on a rack. The meat should not sit directly in the roasting pan, or the liquid dripping from it will braise the underside. The roasting pan should not be larger than necessary, or the meat drippings will spread around and burn, giving the roast an acrid taste and reducing the pan juices, which are the roast's finest gravy. I also think that no oven roast should exceed 6 or 7 pounds. If it is much larger, the outside tends to be over-cooked, whereas the inside is insufficiently done.

PREHEATING THE OVEN. It will always be a mystery to me why people can't understand that there is a world of difference be-tween putting a dish into an oven that's already hot and allowing it to heat up with the oven. Since this simple fact seems so hard to grasp, let me say that, in roasting, it is of the greatest importance that the oven be preheated and really hot, since the heat is to sear the meat and keep the juices inside. The same goes for broiling. The broiler should be as hot as can be (some chefs say this takes 10 min-utes to achieve), and well greased.

SEARING OR NOT SEARING. Searing means placing the roast into a very hot (450° F) oven and leaving it there for 20 to 25 minutes to close its pores and seal in the juices. The oven temperature is then lowered to 300° to 350° F, depending on the meat, and the roast is cooked with frequent bastings of melted fat. This is the old-fashioned way of starting a roast and is decried as obsolete by many moderns. They advocate roasting the meat at *one* low temperature, saying that there is less shrinkage and a more evenly cooked product, and that the fat does not spatter. Having given the arguments for the other side, I now go on record as saying that I think the low-temperature method inferior, except for some bird cookery, and I have the French *haute cuisine* in back of me. Low-temperature cooked meat is tasteless, compared to the other. The economy factor is very small and leaves me stone cold when I think of the other waste in American kitchens. As for the spattering fat, there are several excellent, fast oven cleaners. As to whether all oven-roasted meats should be seared, I agree with those European experts who say, "Yes, even veal, lamb, and poultry." Their juices are not as copious as that of good beef, but that makes them all the more worth preserving.

BASTING. The theory of the French *haute cuisine* and the great English roasting masters (and none are greater) is that meat must be basted, basted frequently, and only with clean fat containing no burned particles. Often it will be necessary to keep melted fat in a dish especially for basting, since the pan drippings may be burned. Stock is permissible for use in basting in some instances, but it is not a classic procedure, one of the reasons being that the water in it will open the meat pores that have been so carefully closed by searing. Another reason is that it will evaporate and cause steam, which consumes the little dry air there is in the oven. However, at times, dry wine, mixed with the pan juices, is used for basting when the meat must be made more flavorsome.

BRAISED MEATS, POT ROASTS, STEWS, AND CASSE-ROLES. These are slow-cooking methods to make the meats tender, using more or less liquid. The liquid in stews is water, wine, or bouillon, or a combination of these, whereas casseroles are cooked in a sauce that's already made. Braised meats, which are extremely popular in all of Europe, are cooked in a minimum of liquid—just enough to generate sufficient steam to cook the meat. All of these processes require pots with extremely tight-fitting lids. The steam must not escape. And they must be simmered over low heat. Simmering can be done in a low oven or over a top burner. An asbestos plate placed over the burner helps tone down the heat and allows true simmering. Since more dishes have been spoiled by misunderstanding of what simmering is, and as a result are boiled instead, let me stress this. A liquid simmers when the movement on the surface is agitated in the gentlest manner, with an occasional bubble here or there. There is no rapid bubbling or strong movement. If that occurs, the liquid is boiling. And boiling ruins the meats that should be simmered (stews and pot roasts), since it toughens them.

Controversy is rampant as to whether the meats for the above dishes should be seared in hot fat. If there is no searing, the juices escape and flavors intermingle in an uninhibited manner, says one school. I adhere to the other, or French, school, which says that all the ingredients, even the vegetables, should be seared or sautéed in fat before the liquid is added, regardless of whether they go into the dish at the very beginning or are added later, as in the case of the tenderer vegetables. They taste better, keep their shape, and the juice of the dish is just as good. However, to be authentic, some national dishes, such as Irish stew, require no searing—and that is that.

A great many cooks labor under the misapprehension that stews, casseroles, or braised meats are, so to speak, timeless, and can be kept cooking at will. They can't. They overcook, just like any other food, though not as spectacularly as a steak or soufflé, since their cooking time is longer. But overcook they do, and the reason that too often few of these dishes are worth eating is that the cook thinks stewing is stewing, and lets the dish continue to cook without considering that chicken or veal do not take as long to stew as beef or mutton, and that their flesh will disintegrate, whereas the other meats will retain their firmness much longer.

LARDING. Talking of larding, it's worthwhile to explain this process, though you will not have to use it for the recipes in this book.

But as a cook, you should be aware of it. Larding is a process that makes dry meat more succulent by the insertion of lardoons—long strips of usually blanched, salted pork or ham about ½ inch wide. This is done with a larding needle (which can be bought in fancy housewares stores) on which the lardoons are threaded and then inserted across the grain of the meat. It immensely improves the flavor if, before use, the lardoons are rolled in salt and pepper, chopped parsley, and a pinch of spice such as cloves or nutmeg, or even soaked in brandy. However, few home cooks are willing to lard at home. They should ask the butcher to lard their pot roasts, and generally he will. The French, masters of pot roasts, are great ones for larding, one of the reasons why pot roast is almost invariably superior in France.

Since larding really makes a world of difference in the succulence and tenderness of the meat, it is worthwhile to acquire a needle and the technique. In a pinch, meat can be larded with an ice pick or a thick knitting needle. You insert the needle into the meat and poke holes for the lardoons. Then you push them in with the ice pick or needle. Keep lardoons in a cold place until needed. However, since American meat is much fattier than European meat, larding is not often necessary and not much practiced by American cooks.

MARINATING. A process by which meat is soaked in wine or vinegar, oil or not, and seasonings. It is used a great deal where the meats are tough, as in Spain, and certainly tenderizes them. However, marinating also impregnates the meat with the flavor of the red or white wine or vinegar in which it was soaked. Some like this flavor, others don't. Before browning, marinated meat must *always* be drained (on a rack set over a bowl), and thoroughly dried (with paper towels) or it won't brown properly.

SIZE OF VESSEL, LIDS, COOKING TIME. Meats cook differently in vessels of different sizes. For the sake of uniformity, the amount of liquid for a dish will be specified, but it may be necessary to increase or decrease this amount depending on the size of the cooking vessel, and to adjust the cooking time accordingly. Cooking utensils are by no means standard, and we must cook in what we have. Fortunately, stews, casseroles, and braised meats are not subject to the deadly accuracy required in baking, where even the smallest deviation in ingredients can cause disaster. The beauty of stews is that they are "more-or-less" dishes as to both quantity and flavoring, subject to the invention and ingenuity of the cook. Damage is easily repaired. If the dish is too liquid, reduce by evaporation—that is, cooking without a cover—or by thickening with a little *beurre manié* (butter and flour kneaded together) with butter alone, or with an extra egg yolk if the dish calls for eggs. If too thick, add more water, wine, or bouillon, whatever the case may be. But be sure the liquid is hot, since sudden temperature changes improve meats no more than they improve human tempers.

Lids must be tight-fitting, so that no steam escapes. Many a dish has been ruined by a loose lid. American cooks are apt to be careless in this respect, and forget that a pan with a truly tight lid is one of the reasons why "things taste so much better in Europe."

Not only the shape and size of the pan but the shape of the meat also affects its cooking time, as do age, quality, and cut. This is the reason that recipes invariably state, after an approximate estimate of cooking time, "until tender."

How much meat to allow for one serving depends entirely on the kind of dish, the kind of meal, and, naturally, the appetite and capacity of the eater. Speaking very roughly, allow a half pound of meat per person; more if the meat is bony, less if it is cut thin as for scaloppine.

As a last word, I should like to stress the importance of serving foods really hot, on heated dishes and plates. Meats, particularly, should always be served on heated plates, since cooling, to put it mildly, does not improve their looks. It is easy enough to heat plates by rinsing them in hot water or standing them on the hot stove or in a warm oven.

Finally, why do I jazz up my meats with capers, vinegar, and so on? To make them livelier, since I don't find meat as tasty as it should be, except when it comes at great cost from a very good butcher.

POT ROAST WITH VINEGAR AND CAPERS

Serves 4 to 6

 2 pounds beef round
½ cup olive oil
⅓ cup wine vinegar
    Salt
    Freshly ground pepper
½ cup capers, drained

Trim all fat from the beef. Place the beef, olive oil, and vinegar in a saucepan that will just hold it and that has a tight-fitting lid. Season with a little salt and pepper. Simmer, covered, over low heat for about 2 hours, or until meat is tender. Cut the beef into slices and arrange them overlapping on a heated serving dish. Ladle a few tablespoons of pan juices over the meat to keep it moist and sprinkle with the capers. Serve hot with mashed potatoes, or cold with a vegetable salad.

NOTE: Chill remaining pan juices and lift off the solidified fat. Use juices for soups, sauces, or stews.

EASY HAMBURGER AND MUSHROOMS IN SOUR CREAM

*A good family standby, also known as good ol' Hamburger
Stroganoff.*

Serves 4

3 tablespoons butter
2 medium onions, thinly sliced
1 pound mushrooms, thinly sliced
1 pound ground round or any lean ground beef
½ teaspoon curry powder, ground ginger, or ground cardamom
  Salt
  Freshly ground pepper
1 cup sour cream or plain yogurt

Heat the butter in a large deep frying pan. Add the onions and cook,
stirring constantly, until soft but not brown. Add the mushrooms.
Cook over medium heat, stirring frequently, until the mushrooms
have released almost all of their liquid, about 8 minutes. Stir in the
ground beef and cook for 2 more minutes. Add the curry powder,
salt and pepper to taste, and the sour cream. Mix well and reduce
the heat. Cook until sour cream is heated through, but do not let boil
or sauce will curdle. Serve immediately with buttered rice or noodles.

SAUERBRATEN

Sauerbraten is a marinated German pot roast whose cooking liquid is thickened with gingersnaps or gingerbread. It is the most popular of all German dishes. The beef can be marinated in either red or white wine, provided the wine is full-bodied. I prefer white wine since it makes for a less acid dish. But suit yourself. Dry the meat thoroughly after removing it from the marinade or it won't brown. Be sure to let the meat marinate 3 to 4 days before cooking and serving.

Serves 6 to 8

MARINADE
1½ cups full-bodied white wine
 ½ cup white vinegar (use red wine vinegar if using red wine)
 1 cup water
 1 large onion, thinly sliced
 1 large carrot, chopped
 1 stalk celery, chopped
 2 bay leaves
 1 teaspoon freshly ground pepper

 1 4-pound boneless beef roast (preferably top or bottom round)
 ¼ cup lard or bacon fat, or 2 tablespoons butter and 2 tablespoons salad oil
 Salt
 Freshly ground pepper
 1 cup crumbled gingersnaps or gingerbread
 ¼ cup heavy cream (optional)

Combine the wine, vinegar, water, onion, carrot, celery, bay leaves, and pepper in a saucepan. Bring to a boil, boil for 1 minute, and cool. Put the beef into a ceramic, Pyrex, or enameled bowl (do not use aluminum) that is just large enough to hold it. Pour the marinade over the beef. The marinade must come about two thirds of the way up the sides of the meat; if necessary, add more wine. Turn the beef in the marinade to moisten all sides. Cover the bowl with plastic wrap or aluminum foil. Refrigerate for 3 to 4 days, turning the beef over twice a day.

Remove the beef from the marinade and dry it thoroughly with paper towels. Strain the marinade into a saucepan and reserve. Heat the lard or other fat in a large, heavy casserole. Brown the beef on all sides over high heat; this will take about 10 minutes. Do not scorch the beef. Transfer the beef to a plate and pour off all the fat in the casserole. Return the beef to the casserole. Bring the marinade to a boil and pour it over the beef. Season with a little salt and pepper. Simmer, tightly covered, over very low heat (or cook in a preheated 300° F oven) for about 2½ to 3 hours, or until beef is tender. Transfer the beef to a heated serving platter and keep warm. Strain the pan juices into a measuring cup; there should be about 2½ cups liquid. If there is more, boil it down; if there is less, add enough hot wine or water to make up the difference. Put the gingersnaps into a small saucepan and strain the pan juices into the crumbs. Mix well, check the seasoning, and bring to a boil. Add the heavy cream. Remove from heat, but keep very hot. Cut the beef into ¼-inch-thick slices and arrange in overlapping layers on the serving platter. Spoon a few tablespoons of the sauce over the meat to keep it moist. Pass the remaining sauce separately. Serve with potatoes or dumplings.

PIQUANT MEATBALLS WITH CAPERS

Serves 4 (15 to 18 meatballs)

1 to 1½ pounds ground beef
2 eggs
¼ cup capers, drained, and chopped if large
⅓ cup freshly grated Parmesan cheese
2 tablespoons fine dry bread crumbs
¾ teaspoon salt
  Freshly ground pepper
½ teaspoon dried marjoram
  Flour
1 tablespoon butter
2 tablespoons olive oil
⅓ to ½ cup dry white wine

Combine the beef, eggs, capers, cheese, bread crumbs, salt, pepper to taste, and marjoram. Mix very thoroughly. With hands dipped in flour, shape the meat mixture into 1½-inch balls. Flatten balls out a little for quicker cooking. Coat meatballs with flour, shaking off excess. Heat the butter and oil in a large frying pan. Cook the meatballs over medium heat for 5 to 7 minutes, turning once (cooking time depends on the thickness and desired doneness of the meat). A few minutes before meatballs are done, sprinkle them with the wine and reduce the heat, letting the meatballs absorb the wine. Serve hot, with the pan juices poured over the meat, or cold. Accompany with a tossed green salad.

SOUR CLOPS

This dish, of Baltic origin, called Koenigsberger Klops *in* Germany, *consists of piquant meatballs in lemon and caper sauce. (*Klops *is a North German word for a meat patty.) I developed this recipe for the* Russian Tea Room Cookbook *(*Richard Marek, 1981*) and use it with the permission of* Faith Stewart Gordon, *who wrote the text of the book.*

Serves 6

MEATBALLS

3 slices white bread, crusts removed
¾ cup milk
2 tablespoons butter
1 small onion, minced
1 pound ground round, ground twice
1 pound lean boneless veal, ground twice
2 anchovy fillets, drained and mashed, or 2 teaspoons anchovy paste
  Grated rind of ½ small lemon
2 eggs, lightly beaten
½ teaspoon salt
¼ teaspoon freshly ground pepper

Soak the bread in the milk until it is thoroughly saturated. With your hands, squeeze the bread dry and reserve. Heat the butter in a small frying pan. Cook the onion over medium heat, stirring constantly, for 3 to 5 minutes, or until soft. Turn all the meat into a large bowl. Add the bread, onion, anchovy fillets, lemon rind, eggs, salt, and pepper. Knead vigorously with both hands until all the ingredients are thoroughly blended. (Moisten your hands occasionally with cold water to prevent sticking.) Using a rounded ¼ cup measure, divide the mixture into 18 portions. With moistened hands, shape each portion into a ball. Place on a platter and refrigerate until cooking time.

POACHING LIQUID
2 quarts beef bouillon (can be made from cubes)
1 medium onion, peeled and stuck with 4 whole cloves
2 bay leaves

Combine all the ingredients in a large heavy saucepan or soup kettle. Bring to a boil and cook over medium heat for 10 minutes. Reduce the heat to low. Carefully drop the meatballs into the poaching liquid. Simmer, uncovered, for 20 to 30 minutes. Transfer the meatballs with a slotted spoon to a deep, heated serving dish. Cover immediately with aluminum foil—meatballs darken when exposed to air. Keep warm in a low oven (150° to 175° F). Strain the poaching liquid into a bowl and reserve.

SAUCE
6 tablespoons butter
6 tablespoons flour
2 cups poaching liquid
1 cup dry white wine
1 tablespoon fresh lemon juice
2 tablespoons capers, drained
2 egg yolks, beaten
2 to 3 tablespoons sour cream
⅓ teaspoon sugar

Heat the butter in a large heavy frying pan. Stir in the flour. Cook over low to medium heat, stirring constantly, for 1 to 2 minutes; the mixture must remain pale. Stir in the poaching liquid and wine. Cook, stirring constantly, until the mixture thickens and is smooth. Reduce the heat to low. Stir in the lemon juice and capers. Cook for about 10 minutes, stirring frequently. Stir about ¼ cup of the sauce into the egg yolks and blend thoroughly. Return mixture to sauce and mix well. Stir in the sour cream and sugar; the sauce should have a touch of sweetness. Add meatballs to sauce. Simmer until they are heated through, basting them frequently with the sauce. Do not let boil or the sauce will curdle. To serve, turn meatballs and sauce into a heated serving dish and serve immediately. Serve with plain boiled potatoes, rice, or noodles to absorb the sauce (rice and noodles may be gently buttered) and buttered string beans.

COLD VEAL WITH TUNA SAUCE

VITELLO TONNATO

This may be an hors d'oeuvre or the main dish of a summer meal with a salad. As with all popular dishes, there are many variations of this famous Italian dish.

Serves 6 to 10

2 tablespoons olive oil
3 to 4 pounds boneless rolled leg of veal
1 large onion, sliced
1 2-ounce can anchovy fillets, drained
⅓ cup minced sour pickle
1 7-ounce can tuna, drained and flaked
1 cup dry white wine
2 cloves garlic, cut in half
2 stalks celery, 1 with leaves, cut into thin slices
1 medium carrot, cut into thin slices
3 sprigs parsley
½ teaspoon dried thyme
1 teaspoon salt
¼ teaspoon freshly ground pepper
2 tablespoons lemon juice
  Mayonnaise
¼ cup capers, drained

Heat the olive oil in a Dutch oven or a deep pot with a tight-fitting lid. Add the veal and over high heat quickly brown very lightly on all sides. Add the onion, anchovy fillets, pickle, tuna, wine, garlic, celery, carrot, parsley, thyme, salt, and pepper. Bring to a boil, skim, and reduce the heat to very low. Simmer, covered, skimming when needed, for about 2 hours, or until veal is tender but not mushy. Remove the veal and place in a large bowl that is not aluminum. Purée pan liquid and vegetables preferably in a blender or food processor until smooth, then pour the mixture over the veal. Cool, cover with plastic wrap, and refrigerate for 8 hours or overnight.

At serving time, remove any fat that has risen to the top. Take out the veal and with a spoon scrape it clean of the marinade. Cut the veal into thin slices and arrange them overlapping on a deep serving platter. Stir the lemon juice into the marinade and thin it with mayonnaise to the consistency of thin cream. Spoon the sauce over veal slices and sprinkle with the capers.

FLORENTINE BROILED BREAST OF VEAL

Serves 4

1 3- to 4-pound breast of veal
2 teaspoons salt
3 whole peppercorns
1 stalk celery
1 carrot
1 onion
1 cup dry white wine
¼ cup olive oil
3 tablespoons fresh lemon juice
   Grated rind of 1 lemon
2 tablespoons chopped parsley
⅛ teaspoon ground nutmeg
1 tablespoon butter, melted
2 large eggs, beaten
   Fine dry bread crumbs

Put the veal into a deep kettle. Add boiling water to cover. Add the salt, peppercorns, celery, carrot, onion, and wine. Simmer, covered, for about 45 minutes, or until veal is tender. Remove veal. Strain liquid and use for soups. Remove and discard all bones and gristle from veal. Place veal on a large platter, cover with another large platter, and weigh down top platter with cans of food, an electric iron, or anything heavy; this will flatten the meat.

In a bowl, combine the olive oil, lemon juice, lemon rind, parsley, and nutmeg. When veal is cool, cut into 1- to 2-inch strips. Put strips into marinade and let stand for 2 hours at room temperature, or refrigerate if it is very hot, turning occasionally so that the marinade can penetrate the meat on all sides. Dry strips between paper towels. Combine the butter and eggs. Dip strips into the mixture, then coat with bread crumbs. Place meat strips in 1 layer on broiler pan. Broil under medium heat until golden, then turn and broil on other side. Line a heated serving dish with a napkin and arrange meat on it; this will keep the meat hot. Serve immediately with a tartar or green sauce and a vegetable salad.

NOTE: The marinated veal strips may also be placed in a greased shallow baking dish in 1 layer and baked in a preheated 375° F oven for 15 minutes, or until golden. Turn and bake for 10 more minutes.

———

FANCY VEAL CUTLETS BASQUAISE

Serves 6

¼ cup oil (preferably olive)
6 veal cutlets (about 1 pound, 2 ounces), dried thoroughly on both sides
3 medium onions, peeled and thinly sliced (2 to 2½ cups)
3 medium sweet green peppers, quartered lengthwise, then sliced thinly crosswise (3 cups)
¼ cup dry white wine
¼ cup brandy
1 28-ounce can whole tomatoes, very well drained, then coarsely chopped (1½ cups), or equivalent amount peeled, seeded, and coarsely chopped fresh tomatoes (about 3 medium)
  Salt
  Freshly ground pepper
2 tablespoons butter
3 veal or mild American or German beef sausages (10 to 12 ounces)
6 thin slices dried cured ham such as Westphalian, prosciutto, or Bayonne, shredded

Heat the oil in a large heavy frying pan. Add 3 of the veal cutlets. Quickly cook cutlets over medium-high heat until lightly browned on both sides, about 3 to 4 minutes, turning once. Remove cutlets to a heated serving dish and keep warm. Add the 3 remaining cutlets to the hot oil. Repeat browning procedure, then remove cutlets to serving dish. Add the onions and peppers to remaining oil in pan. Cook over medium-high heat for about 15 minutes, or until onions and peppers are tender, stirring occasionally and reducing heat as necessary. Stir in the wine and brandy. Stir in the tomatoes and bring to a boil. Reduce the heat to low and cook uncovered for about 5 to 10 minutes, or until some of the tomato liquid has evaporated, stirring occasionally. Season with salt and pepper to taste. Spoon sauce over cutlets, cover with a lid or aluminum foil and keep warm in a very low oven (140° to 175° F). In same pan, heat the butter.

Add the sausages. Cook over medium to low heat for about 5 to 10 minutes until evenly browned, turning frequently. Split sausages in half lengthwise. Top each cutlet with a sausage half. Sprinkle on shredded ham. Serve at once, accompanied by a tossed green salad.

SWISS VEAL IN CREAM SAUCE

I make this just before the guests come, covering the serving dish tightly with foil. I keep the dish warm in a very low oven; if your oven does not turn to 140°–175° F, turn it to the lowest possible setting and keep the oven door ajar or half open.

Serves 4

1½ pounds boneless veal (preferably from the leg), in 1 piece
    Salt
    Freshly ground pepper
    Juice of 1 lemon or 2 tablespoons brandy
¼ cup butter
1 cup chicken bouillon
½ cup heavy cream
    Paprika

Cut the veal into ½-inch-thick slices; they should all be the same size. Lay on a platter, and sprinkle with salt and pepper to taste, and the lemon juice. Let stand for 10 minutes at room temperature. Heat the butter in a large frying pan. Cook the veal slices for 3 minutes on each side, or until golden brown. Transfer the slices to a heated serving dish and keep warm in a low oven. Stir the consommé into the pan juices, scraping up all the brown bits at the bottom of the pan. Bring to a boil and reduce by about one fourth. Reduce the heat and stir in the cream. Cook sauce until shiny and the consistency of heavy cream. Pour sauce over veal and sprinkle with paprika. Serve with Swiss Fried Potato Cake, page 215.

MY MOTHER'S ROAST LEG OF LAMB

Serves 8 to 10

1 6- to 7-pound leg of lamb
8 cloves garlic, minced
2 cups parsley sprigs, freshly washed and chopped while still damp
½ cup fresh rosemary leaves or ¼ cup dried rosemary, crumbled
Salt
Freshly ground pepper
Olive oil
Dry white wine

Preheat the oven to hot (400° F).

Trim every bit of fat, gristle, and fell (skin) from the lamb. The meat must be totally bare; this is essential for the flavor of the dish. (It takes time and patience, and you will be surprised how much waste there is on a leg of lamb; most likely, you will be trimming off more than 1 pound of fat.) The meat will partially hang in loose folds, but it will be tied up for cooking. Tie the meat with kitchen string. Mince together the garlic, parsley, and rosemary until they are almost a paste; the dampness of the parsley will make the ingredients stick together. With a sharp knife, make little pockets all over the lamb. Push a little of the garlic mixture into each pocket, using the point of a knife. Rub the lamb with salt and pepper, and with your hands spread on a generous coating of olive oil; in fact massage the meat with the oil. (The lamb can be cooked immediately, but it will be more flavorful if wrapped in plastic wrap and refrigerated overnight.) Put the lamb on a rack in a roasting pan and add 1 inch of wine. Roast for 15 minutes. Reduce the heat to 325° F and roast for about 3 hours, or until tender. Baste frequently with the pan juices. When they run dry, add more wine, but no more than 1 inch. Do not add any wine during the last 30 minutes of roasting because the leg of lamb should be dry when finished. Serve warm or cool but not chilled, with a simple potato salad.

LAMB STEW WITH EGG SAUCE

I have also used this recipe with veal, in an unorthodox manner, and it comes out very well.

Serves 4 to 6

      2 pounds boneless lamb or veal
     ¼ cup minced prosciutto or lean bacon
      2 tablespoons minced onion
    1½ tablespoons lard
         Salt
         Freshly ground pepper
      2 tablespoons flour
     ½ cup dry white wine
      3 egg yolks
    1½ tablespoons fresh lemon juice
     ¼ cup minced parsley
     ½ teaspoon dried marjoram

Trim the lamb of all excess fat and cut into 1½-inch cubes. In a deep skillet or saucepan, combine the lamb, prosciutto, onion, and lard. Cook over medium heat, stirring constantly, until lamb is golden; it should not be brown. Season with salt and pepper to taste, and sprinkle with the flour. Cook for 2 minutes longer. Add the wine and cook, stirring frequently, until the wine has evaporated. Add hot water to almost cover the meat. Simmer, covered, over low heat, stirring frequently, for 35 minutes, or until meat is tender. If necessary, add a little more hot water to prevent scorching. About 10 minutes before serving time, beat together the egg yolks, lemon juice, parsley, and marjoram. Remove lamb from heat and stir in egg sauce. Keep in a warm place, but not over direct heat, until the sauce has set without curdling, about 5 minutes.

SPICY MOROCCAN LAMB CASSEROLE

Serves 6

- 3 tablespoons butter
- 2 pounds lean lamb or beef, cut into 2-inch strips
- 1 large onion, minced
- 2 cloves garlic, mashed
- 2 tablespoons flour
- 1½ cups chicken or beef bouillon
- ½ teaspoon saffron, powdered or in threads
- ½ teaspoon cardamom seeds or ground cardamom
- ⅛ teaspoon ground ginger
- 1¼ teaspoons ground cinnamon, or less to taste
- ⅔ cup golden raisins
  Salt
  Freshly ground pepper
- 2 or 3 small yellow squash, peeled and cubed
  Juice of 1 lemon

Heat the butter in a frying pan. Brown the meat well on all sides over high heat. Transfer meat to a 3-quart casserole. Reduce the heat to medium, and cook the onion and garlic in the pan juices until the onion is tender. Stir in the flour and cook for 3 minutes longer, stirring constantly. The mixture should be medium brown. Add the bouillon, saffron, cardamom, ginger, cinnamon, raisins, and salt and pepper to taste, and toss with the meat. Simmer, covered, over low heat, stirring constantly, for 45 minutes, or until meat is almost tender. Add the squash and cook until meat and squash are tender, about 5 to 10 minutes. Remove the casserole from the heat and stir in the lemon juice. Serve this spicy North African dish with cracked wheat pilaff and leeks vinaigrette.

CHINA CHILO

An old dish from the British East India Company days, extremely simple and very pleasant. It is the best way of using up the bits and pieces of a defunct roast leg of lamb.

Serves 3 or 4

About 1 pound leftover rare roast lamb,
  chopped fine (2 to 3 cups)
2 small heads or 1 large head romaine lettuce, shredded
1 large red onion, thinly sliced and separated into rings
¾ cup chicken bouillon (can be made with cube) or water
¼ cup butter
⅛ teaspoon ground ginger and/or mace (optional)
  Salt
  Freshly ground pepper
1 10-ounce package frozen peas, cooked and drained
1 medium cucumber, peeled, seeded, and cut into 1½-inch
  pieces

In a large casserole that can go to the table, combine the lamb, lettuce, onion, bouillon, butter, ginger, and salt and pepper to taste. Simmer, covered, over very low heat for about 30 to 40 minutes. Stir in the peas and heat through thoroughly. Before serving, add the cucumber pieces and mix well. Serve very hot, with chutney on the side.

NOTE: If you like a hotter dish, add Tabasco to taste.

PORK ARISTA

A dish that dates back to the Renaissance. Arista is a way of seasoning and cooking; I have also made this dish successfully with a boned veal roast or a leg of lamb.

Serves 6 to 8

1 4-pound loin of pork, cut to form chops but not cut through backbone
4 large cloves garlic, peeled and cut into quarters
3 tablespoons fresh rosemary leaves, or 1 to 2 tablespoons dried rosemary, crumbled
4 whole cloves
Salt
Freshly ground pepper
Olive oil
Dry white wine

Preheat the oven to slow (300° F).

Trim all excess fat from the pork. Wet the garlic pieces in water and roll them in the rosemary leaves to coat. Insert some of the garlic quarters between the chops, together with the cloves. With a sharp knife, cut small slits in the pork and stuff each slit with garlic. Rub the pork with salt and pepper. With your hands, rub a thin film of olive oil on the pork. Place the meat on a rack in a roasting pan. Add about 2 inches of wine. Roast, allowing 45 minutes roasting time per pound, basting occasionally with the pan juices. Cool the meat to lukewarm in its own juice; it should be moist. Slice and serve with a vegetable salad.

NOTE: Pour the pan juices into a bowl and chill. Remove any fat that has risen to the top and use juices as a sauce for spaghetti or rice.

BONELESS PORK ROAST MARINATED IN WHITE WINE

A triumph of French Provençal cooking. I found the recipe years ago in Family Circle *magazine and have been making it ever since. A 4½-pound loin of pork leaves about 3 pounds of solid meat after boning. The roast tastes good with white beans or flageolets.*

Serves 6 to 8

  1 center cut loin of pork (about 4¼ pounds)
1½ to 2 cups dry white wine
  ½ cup white wine vinegar
  1 large onion, thinly sliced
  2 cloves garlic, chopped
 10 whole peppercorns
  1 teaspoon dried thyme, crumbled
  2 bay leaves, crumbled
  1 teaspoon salt
  ½ teaspoon freshly ground pepper (preferably white pepper)

Ask the butcher to bone the loin of pork and give you the bones (you will roast the bones with the pork). Tie the pork at 2-inch intervals with kitchen string to keep the compact shape.

Combine the wine, vinegar, onion, garlic, peppercorns, thyme, and bay leaves in a nonmetal bowl just large enough to hold the meat. Place pork and bones into the marinade, meat side down. Cover and refrigerate overnight or for 24 hours. Drain the meat, reserving the marinade, and scrape off vegetables and spices. Sprinkle with the salt and pepper.

Preheat the oven to moderate (325° F). Place pork and bones in a roasting pan. Add ½ cup of the marinade, including the onion and garlic, to the meat. Roast for about 1½ hours, allowing 30 minutes roasting time per pound, or until a meat thermometer inserted into the meaty part of the roast registers 170°; the point of the thermometer should not rest in fat. Baste occasionally with the marinade. Transfer the meat to a heated serving dish and keep warm. Pour off all the fat, but leave the brown bits at the bottom of the roasting pan. Add about ½ cup of the remaining marinade, scraping up all the brown bits. Bring to a boil and turn off the heat. Keep warm. Cut the pork into slices and arrange them overlapping on a heated platter or serving dish. Spoon the pan juices over the meat. There should be just enough sauce to keep the meat moist and flavorful; this is not a sauced dish. Serve hot, with the bones on another serving platter; they may be eaten with the fingers, provided there are enough napkins! Or if you have fingerbowls, now is the time to use them.

PORK TENDERLOIN WITH MADEIRA

A party dish from Denmark, where Madeira is a must in the kitchen.

Serves 4 to 6

1 1½- to 2-pound pork tenderloin, trimmed of all fat
3 tablespoons butter
2 medium onions, finely chopped
  Salt
  Freshly ground pepper
1 to 1½ cups Madeira
½ pound fresh mushrooms, sliced
2 tablespoons flour
1 cup light cream

Preheat the oven to moderate (350° F).

Cut the pork tenderloin into 6 to 8 slices. Heat 2 tablespoons of the butter in a skillet. Brown the pork slices over high heat for 1 to 2 minutes on each side. Transfer the slices to a heavy casserole. Brown the onions in the skillet juices. Spread the onions over the meat. Sprinkle with salt and pepper to taste, and add the Madeira. Bring to a boil, then remove from the heat. Cover and bake for about 1 to 1¼ hours.

While the meat is cooking, heat the remaining tablespoon butter in a skillet and sauté the mushrooms. Add the mushrooms to the pork 15 minutes before the meat is ready. Stir the flour into the cream to make a smooth paste. When the meat is ready, turn off the oven. Carefully transfer the slices to a heated serving dish with a slotted spoon and keep warm in the oven. Stir the cream mixture into the juices in the casserole. Cook, stirring constantly, over lowest possible heat for about 2 to 3 minutes, or until heated through thoroughly, but do not let boil. Pour the sauce over the meat and serve hot. Serve with home-fried potatoes and a green vegetable.

FRENCH PORK CHOPS WITH APPLES

French home cooking.

Serves 4 to 6

5 tablespoons butter
  About 3 Golden Delicious apples (½ pound each),
  cored and each cut into 6 ¼-inch slices (do not peel)
6 boneless loin pork chops, ½ to ¾ inch thick (about 1½ pounds),
  patted dry
2 tablespoons minced shallots
1 cup dry white wine
1 tablespoon Dijon mustard
  Salt
  Cayenne pepper
  Minced parsley

Heat 1 tablespoon of the butter in a large heavy frying pan. Add 6
apple slices and cook over medium heat until golden brown on both
sides, about 5 minutes, turning once. Remove to a heated platter and
keep warm. Cook remaining apple slices the same way, using 1 tablespoon butter for each batch. In the same pan, heat the remaining
2 tablespoons butter. Add the pork chops and brown on both sides
over medium-high heat for about 10 minutes, turning once. Reduce
the heat to low. Cover and cook for 10 to 15 more minutes, or until
chops are tender and no longer pink in center. Remove chops to
platter with apples. Add the shallots and wine to drippings in pan.
Bring to a boil and boil over high heat until liquid is reduced by half
(¾ cup), about 5 minutes. Reduce the heat to low. Stir in the mustard. Season with salt and cayenne pepper to taste. Spoon sauce over
chops and apple slices. Garnish with parsley.

PORK SAUSAGES WITH ORANGES

A basic recipe, or rather, cooking method.

Cooked this way, the sausages will have a delicious light orange flavor. Puncture each sausage with a fork and place in a skillet. Add orange juice to cover and bring to a boil. Reduce the heat and simmer for about 5 minutes, then drain off liquid. Return skillet to heat and cook sausages slowly until evenly browned.

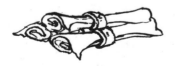

HAM STEAKS IN RUM

Serves 4 or 5

2 ½-inch-thick ham steaks (about 1 pound each)
2 tablespoons brown sugar
2 teaspoons ground ginger
1 teaspoon water
1 cup pineapple juice
1 cup dark rum

Preheat the oven to moderate (350° F).

Trim the ham steaks and place side by side in a buttered baking dish. Mix together the sugar, ginger, and water to make a smooth paste. Spread the paste over ham. Combine the pineapple juice and rum and pour over ham. Bake for about 30 minutes, or until the sauce has thickened. Serve from the baking dish or transfer to a heated serving platter and spoon sauce over the ham.

COLD JELLIED HAM
WITH PARSLEY

JAMBON PERSILLÉ

Standard French, also very pretty as well as tasty. Good for parties.

Serves 10 to 12

3 envelopes (3 tablespoons) unflavored gelatin
5 cups chicken bouillon or 4 cups chicken bouillon and 1 cup dry white wine
   About 2 pounds chilled ham, cut into ⅛-inch cubes or smaller (6 cups) (see Note)
½ cup firmly packed finely chopped parsley (be sure parsley is well dried)
   Parsley sprigs (optional)

Chill a 9x5x3-inch loaf pan. In a small bowl, soften the gelatin in ½ cup of the chicken bouillon. In a large saucepan, bring the remaining 4½ cups (or 3½ cups if using wine) bouillon to a boil. Add softened gelatin and stir until dissolved. If using wine, add now. Chill until mixture thickens slightly. Pour ½ cup gelatin mixture into chilled loaf pan. Top evenly with 3 cups of the ham. Pour on 1½ cups of the gelatin mixture, spreading gelatin evenly. Sprinkle on ¼ cup of the parsley, pressing it gently into gelatin. Cover with ¼ cup of the gelatin mixture. Cover with the remaining 3 cups ham, spreading ham evenly. Evenly pour on the remaining gelatin mixture. Sprinkle on the remaining ¼ cup parsley, pressing it gently into gelatin. Chill overnight. To serve, unmold and cut into slices. Garnish with parsley sprigs if desired.

NOTE: Unless the ham is cut into very small pieces, the ham loaf will crumble in slicing.

SAUTÉED KIDNEYS

Some people don't like kidneys. If treated as in the recipe below, kidneys assume a new dimension that will appeal to non-kidney enthusiasts.

Serves 4

4 veal kidneys
¼ cup butter
1 tablespoon olive oil
½ cup thinly sliced onions or shallots
½ to ¾ cup full-bodied dry red wine
  Salt
  Freshly ground pepper
¼ cup minced parsley

Snip the white membrane and all the fat off the kidneys. Cut kidneys into ¾-inch slices. Put slices into a bowl and cover with cold water. Let stand for 30 minutes to 1 hour at room temperature (refrigerate if it is very hot). Drain thoroughly and return to bowl. Cover with boiling water, let stand for 1 minute, and drain thoroughly. Heat the butter and oil in a skillet. Add the onion and cook until golden. Add kidney slices and cook, stirring frequently, for about 3 minutes. Add the wine and bring to a boil. Reduce the heat and cook for about 5 minutes longer, or until the meat is barely tender. Do not overcook or the kidneys will be tough. Season with salt and pepper to taste, and sprinkle with parsley before serving on toast or buttered rice.

SWEETBREADS TRIAMON

MÉDAILLON DE RIS DE VEAU TRIAMON

French and fancy, but good.

Serves 6

- 3 pair sweetbreads (about 1½ pounds)
- 2 ounces cooked ham, in 1 piece, cut into ½-inch squares, ¼ inch thick
- 3 truffles, cut into eighths (optional)
  Flour
- 2 large eggs, beaten
- ¾ cup fine fresh bread crumbs
- 7 tablespoons butter
- 6 ounces mushrooms, finely chopped
- 3 tablespoons minced shallots
- 2 tablespoons flour
- 1 cup milk
- ½ cup heavy cream
  Salt

Place the sweetbreads in a large saucepan and add cold water to cover. Bring to a boil and boil gently without a cover over low heat for 2 minutes. Drain. Cool under cold running water. Drain well. With a kitchen shears or a knife, trim sweetbreads of all membranes and veins. Place sweetbreads between several layers of paper towel and cover with an inverted plate. Weigh plate down (use a heavy can or two) for 30 minutes. (This procedure flattens sweetbreads slightly and extracts some juices, making them firmer and easier to handle.) With a sharp knife, make several slits in each sweetbread half. Insert the ham squares, and truffle pieces if desired, into slits. Dredge with flour. Dip sweetbreads in the eggs, then coat with the bread crumbs. Heat 4 tablespoons of the butter in a large heavy frying pan. Cook sweetbreads over medium-high heat for about 10 minutes, or until golden brown on both sides, turning once and regulating heat as necessary. Reduce the heat to low. Cook for 10 more minutes until sweetbreads are tender and done, turning once. Remove sweetbreads, set aside and keep warm.

Wash the frying pan. Melt the remaining 3 tablespoons butter. Cook the mushrooms and shallots over medium-high heat for 5 minutes, or until mushrooms are tender, stirring frequently. Reduce the heat to low. Add the flour. Cook for 2 minutes, stirring constantly. Stir in the milk and cream. Cook over low heat, stirring constantly, until sauce thickens and is smooth. Season with salt to taste. To serve, spoon some sauce into a heated serving dish. Place sweetbreads on top. Top with remaining sauce.

SWEETBREADS IN PUFF PASTRY

RIS DE VEAU SAVOYARDE

Some trouble to make, but worth it. I always use frozen patty shells for rolling out, since it is too much trouble to make puff pastry from scratch, at least for me. If you do make your own puff pastry, however, make 10 ounces of it.

Serves 6

3 pair sweetbreads (about 1½ pounds)
Flour
7 tablespoons butter
1 pound mushrooms, whole if small, quartered if medium, cut into eighths if large
¼ cup minced shallots
½ cup dry white wine
¼ cup Madeira
1 cup heavy cream
2 tablespoons flour mixed with 2 tablespoons cold water and blended until smooth
Salt
Freshly ground pepper
1 10-ounce package frozen patty shells, thawed
1 egg, beaten

Place the sweetbreads in a large saucepan and add cold water to cover. Bring to a boil and boil gently over low heat for 2 minutes. Drain. Cool under cold running water. Drain well. With a kitchen shears or a knife and your fingers, trim sweetbreads of all membranes and veins. Place sweetbreads between several layers of paper towel and cover with an inverted plate. Weigh plate down (use a heavy can or two) for 30 minutes. (This procedure flattens sweetbreads slightly and extracts some juices, making them firmer and easier to handle.) Dredge with flour. Heat 4 tablespoons of the butter in a large heavy frying pan until bubbly. Cook sweetbreads over medium-high heat for about 10 minutes, or until golden brown on both sides, turning once and regulating heat as necessary. Remove sweetbreads and set aside.

Add the remaining 3 tablespoons butter to drippings and heat until bubbly. Cook the mushrooms and shallots over medium-high heat for 3 to 5 minutes, or until mushrooms are tender, stirring frequently. Do not overcook. Sir in the white wine and Madeira. Return sweetbreads to pan and bring to a boil. Reduce the heat to low. Simmer for 10 minutes, or until flavors are blended, turning sweetbreads once. Stir in the heavy cream and flour mixture. Simmer just until sauce thickens. Season with salt and pepper to taste. Transfer sweetbreads to a lightly buttered shallow 2-quart casserole.

Preheat the oven to hot (400° F). Stack the 6 patty shells on a work surface and press edges together. Roll out pastry to a size 1 inch larger than dimensions of top of casserole. Place pastry on top of casserole over sweetbread mixture. Press edges of pastry firmly to edges of dish to seal tightly. Make several slits in pastry. Brush pastry with some of the egg. Place casserole on a baking sheet and bake for 20 to 25 minutes, or until pastry is golden brown. To serve, spoon out onto heated serving plates. Serve by itself, with a salad to follow.

Curries

I make my curries the Anglo way, which is not the orthodox Indian way where the cook combines and even grinds her/his own spices. Instead, in the Anglo way I learned long ago in England from an ancient colonel of the Indian Army, I use a good, imported curry powder, preferably Madras curry powder. But I never use the poor little curry powders in the little cans that prevail in supermarkets, because they have practically no flavor. A good imported curry powder is easy to find in any fancy food shop, and heaven knows, they now abound throughout our nation. My curries are tasty, my friends and I think, easier to make and more controllable as to their pungency than the "echt" Indian ones, when these are made by the curry amateur. However, if you wish for the orthodox Indian curries, you have to consult an Indian cookbook, or a cookbook of the cuisines of countries that make a point of curries, such as Thailand and Indonesia. But any way you make your curries, the spices or powder must be of a good quality and fresh, best bought in small quantities because all spices age quickly and lose their flavor. After all, a curry only tastes as good as the powder or spices you use.

Whether you buy your curry powder or make it yourself as the true cognoscenti do, keep in mind that a pinch of curry powder adds an intriguing flavor to many American favorites, from soups to salted nuts, where a tiny bit is added to the salt. The French especially use a pinch of curry powder to flavor white sauces, plain buttered vegetables, and salad dressings, a practice worth imitating when done with a light hand, tasting as one keeps on adding curry powder to one's cooking.

When making a curry proper, remember that the spices should be cooked first in any kind of fat—butter, oil, lard, or even, heaven forbid, margarine. *Do not* use olive oil because of the pronounced flavor; curry oil should be neutral. Onions and garlic must be finely chopped and cooked only until soft; they must not brown or they will spoil the taste of the dish. Curries are best with an acid added to them, such as tamarind juice (as in India), or lemon or lime juice here at home. Curries can be cooked in any kind of utensil and over any kind of heat.

Coconut milk or coconut cream are standard ingredients of many curries but not of all. I may be wrong, but I think that coconut milk is found in most Eastern curries because it tempers the fierceness of the spices and because it is readily available. I like the flavor; it makes good gravies and sauces, but I do not like coconut to be the dominant flavor. The charm of curry is the blend of flavors, and since you have to have a lot of practice and the proper feeling for the role of each spice in a curry to achieve this harmony, I mostly leave the combining of curry spices to others.

How hot a curry? It is a matter of taste. Talking from my own experience, it is better not to make a hot or very spicy dish unless you know it will be liked. My husband does not like hot curries, so I make ours (for family use) on the mild side, and spice mine up (since I like hot foods) with a hot pepper sauce like Tabasco. And since curry is also a state of mind (authentic versus adapted, etc.), I suggest that you do not present guests with a curry dinner unless you are sure, I repeat *sure*, that they are going to like it. Or you'll be left with a lot of uneaten food, prepared at a quite considerable cost of time and ingredients, as I once or twice found out to my sorrow.

———

How to Make Coconut Cream and Milk from Fresh Coconuts

This is a fairly laborious process, but it's worth it, for no dried or preserved coconut can approach the flavor of fresh coconut. The milk can be frozen successfully. Choose only coconuts that are full of liquid; test this by rattling them.

Preheat the oven to moderate (375° F).

With an icepick, puncture the soft spots in 2 of the coconut's eyes. Drain out the liquid and reserve it. Lay the coconut in a pie plate or baking dish. Bake for 15 to 30 minutes; ideally, by that time, it should have cracked. Remove from the oven. Tap the coconut with a meat mallet or a hammer until the shell comes off. Cut the meat into ½-inch cubes; for making coconut cream you need not peel off the brown inner skin. Measure the coconut meat. Measure the coconut liquid and add enough boiling water to the coconut liquid to make the same amount as there is coconut meat. Put 1 cup coconut meat and 1 cup liquid into a blender or food processor. Whirl first at slow speed and then at high speed until the mixture is finely shredded. Drain into a bowl through a double layer of cheesecloth or a clean kitchen towel, twisting and squeezing out as much liquid as possible. Repeat the process until all the coconut meat and liquid are used up. If you do not have a blender, grate the coconut meat into a bowl and add the liquid. Process as above. This is the first squeezing, which makes the thickest cream. For the second, which produces a more diluted liquid, save the squeezed-out coconut and put it into a bowl. Add enough boiling water to barely cover the coconut. Squeeze out as above. Pour the coconut milk into a container and refrigerate. The cream will rise to the top as with cow's milk. Either shake the top cream and the bottom milk together to homogenize them (as for coconut custard) or use separately, depending on the recipe.

How to Make Coconut Cream and Milk from Dried Coconut

Most dried coconut flakes are preserved in a great deal of sugar. This is all right for desserts, but it interferes with other cooking. It is possible to get unsweetened coconut flakes in health and specialty stores, but the sweetened kind is far more prevalent. If you can't find any other kind of coconut flakes, rinse the sweetened variety under cold running water and drain it thoroughly. This will remove part of the sugar.

About 1 cup coconut cream

1½ cups flaked coconut
1½ cups milk

Combine the coconut with the milk. Scald the mixture and let stand for 15 minutes. Squeeze through a double layer of cheesecloth or a clean kitchen towel. This is the first squeezing, which produces the thickish cream. Repeat the process for the second squeezing, which will produce a thin liquid.

BASIC CURRY SAUCE FOR MEATS AND VEGETABLES

About 3 to 4 cups

1 tablespoon butter
4 slices lean bacon, minced
1 medium, onion, minced
1 small clove garlic, minced
2 to 4 tablespoons curry powder, depending on strength and taste
2 tablespoons flour
1 tart apple, unpeeled, cored and chopped, or 1 large pear
¼ cup preserved kumquats or bitter orange marmalade
1 tablespoon honey or 1 teaspoon sugar
1 tablespoon tomato paste
½ cup golden raisins
½ to ⅔ cup chopped dried apricots
1 cup thin coconut milk
1 cup chicken bouillon or 2 cups chicken bouillon
Grated rind of 1 lemon
2 tablespoons fresh lemon juice
Salt
Freshly ground pepper

Combine the butter, bacon, onion, and garlic in a heavy saucepan. Cook over medium heat, stirring constantly, until the onion is soft; do not let it brown. Add the curry powder and cook, stirring constantly, for 3 minutes. Stir in the flour. Add the apple, kumquats, honey, tomato paste, raisins, apricots, coconut milk, chicken bouillon, lemon rind, and 1 tablespoon of the lemon juice. Mix well. Season with salt and pepper to taste. Simmer, covered, over medium heat for 25 minutes, stirring frequently. If you like a thicker sauce, uncover for the final 10 minutes of cooking. When cooked, stir in the remaining tablespoon lemon juice. Let cool, then purée in a blender or food processor.

NOTE: This sauce will freeze well.

FRUIT CURRY SAUCE

Different—not hot—and full of subtle flavors thanks to the fruit. On the acid side. The coconut milk can be omitted, but the flavor won't be the same.

About 4 cups

1 medium onion, minced
½ cup cooked ham, minced
2 slices bacon, minced
4 tablespoons curry powder
1 tablespoon flour
Juice of 2 lemons
1 tart apple, unpeeled, cored and chopped
½ cup preserved kumquats or bitter orange marmalade
1 tablespoon tomato paste
2 tablespoons honey
Salt
Freshly ground pepper
1 cup chicken bouillon
2 cups thick coconut milk
1 cup grated or shredded unsweetened coconut, fresh or dried

Combine the onion, ham, and bacon in a heavy saucepan. Cook over medium heat, stirring constantly, until the onion is soft. Sprinkle with the curry powder and cook, stirring constantly, for 2 more minutes. Stir in the flour. Add the juice of 1 lemon, the apple, kumquats, tomato paste, and honey, and mix well. Season lightly with salt and pepper. Stir in the chicken bouillon and coconut milk, and coconut. Bring to a boil, reduce the heat, and simmer, covered, for 30 minutes. Stir occasionally. Check the seasoning. Remove from heat and stir in the remaining lemon juice. Let cool, then puree in a blender or food processor. Refrigerate for up to a week, or freeze.

NOTE: The thickness of any sauce is a matter of preference. Therefore, either reduce this curry sauce by simmering it without a cover to allow for evaporation, or thin it with a little more chicken bouillon.

VICTORIAN CREAM CURRY

This curry should be on the mild side, appealing to people who do not like curries.

Serves 4 or 5

3 chicken breasts, cut in half
¼ cup butter
1 medium onion, minced
4 shallots, minced
1 tablespoon curry powder
1 tablespoon flour
1 to 1½ cups heavy cream
   Salt
   Freshly ground pepper
1 tablespoon fresh lemon juice (optional)

Preheat the oven to hot (400° F).

Remove the skin, fat, and center bone from the chicken breasts. Heat 2 tablespoons of the butter in a skillet and cook the chicken breasts until golden, but do not brown. Transfer the chicken breasts to an ovenproof casserole. Add the remaining 2 tablespoons butter to the skillet, and cook the onion and shallots until soft and golden. Stir in the curry powder and cook, stirring constantly, for 3 minutes. Stir in the flour and cook for 1 minute longer. Transfer the mixture to the casserole, spooning it between and over the chicken breasts. Add 1 cup of the cream. Season with salt and pepper to taste. Bake, covered, for about 15 to 20 minutes, depending on the size of the chicken breasts. Check while baking; if sauce is too thick, add the remaining ½ cup cream. The sauce should have the consistency of thick cream. Remove from the oven. Stir in the lemon juice if desired. Serve with saffron rice, a green vegetable such as peas or green beans, and Lemon Chutney, page 246, or Lemon Compote, page 248.

BEEF, LAMB, OR PORK CURRY

The recipe may be halved.

Serves 8

3 to 4 pounds lean stewing beef, such as round, or boneless lamb
   or pork
¼ cup salad oil
1 recipe Fruit Curry Sauce, page 194

Cut the meat into 1-inch pieces and trim off every bit of fat and gristle. Heat 2 tablespoons of the oil in a large heavy skillet. Brown half the meat (or less) over high heat; do not crowd the pieces. Transfer the browned pieces to a large heavy casserole or saucepan. Add the remaining 2 tablespoons oil to the skillet and brown the remaining meat, then add to the casserole. Add the Fruit Curry Sauce and mix well. Bring to a boil and reduce the heat. Simmer, covered, for 1 hour or until the meat is tender. Check the seasoning. Adjust the thickness of the sauce by either simmering it without a cover to allow for evaporation, or thin it by adding a little hot water, bouillon, or coconut milk. Serve with Pilaff of Rice with Raisins and Pine Nuts, page 89.

GOLDEN LAMB CURRY

Serves 6 to 8

1 to 2 cups plain yogurt
1 cup thin coconut milk
4 green onions, minced
  Salt
  Freshly ground pepper
3 pounds lean lamb, cut into 1½-inch cubes
3 tablespoons butter
1 tablespoon flour
1 recipe Basic Curry Sauce for Meats and Vegetables, page 193
¾ cup golden raisins (optional)
  Apricot jam, bitter orange marmalade, or lemon juice (optional)

In a deep nonaluminum bowl, combine the yogurt, coconut milk, and green onions, and add salt and pepper to taste. Mix thoroughly. Cut every bit of gristle, fat, and skin from the lamb; the total absence of these influences the taste of lamb most favorably. Put the lamb into the yogurt mixture and stir it around, so that the pieces are well coated. Cover and refrigerate for 24 hours, turning the lamb once or twice. Drain the meat, reserving the marinade, and dry the pieces with paper towels. Heat the butter in a deep skillet. Brown the lamb over high heat. Transfer the browned pieces to a deep saucepan or casserole. Stir the flour into the lamb. Add the Basic Curry Sauce, and the raisins if desired. Bring to a boil. Reduce the heat, cover, and simmer over lowest possible heat for about 1 hour. Check the seasoning. Stir occasionally and watch the thickness of the sauce. If you like a thinner sauce, add some of the reserved yogurt marinade, a little at a time. Taste for flavor, adding a little apricot jam, orange marmalade, or lemon juice after the dish is cooked. Do not let boil or it may curdle.

MALAY CURRY

The ingredients for this curry are freshly ground, hence no curry powder is used. It is spicy rather than hot, but it can be made hotter with the addition of Tabasco and/or red chili pepper. One inch of fresh hot chili pepper, seeded and minced, is quite hot.

Serves 8

SPICE MIXTURE
- 10 whole peppercorns
- ½ teaspoon ground cumin or cumin seeds
- 1 teaspoon caraway or fennel seeds
- 1 teaspoon coriander seeds or ½ teaspoon ground coriander
- 1 teaspoon ground tumeric
- ½ teaspoon grated nutmeg
- Grated rind of 1 large lemon
- 3 tablespoons minced fresh gingerroot or 1 tablespoon ground ginger
- 4 cloves garlic, chopped
- 8 blanched almonds or 6 cashews
- 1 to 2 tablespoons salad oil

Put all the ingredients with 1 tablespoon of the salad oil into a blender or food processor. Or use a mortar and pestle. Blend to a paste, scraping down sides with a rubber spatula. Add more oil if mixture is too thick and does not purée. Transfer paste to a small bowl and reserve.

ASSEMBLING THE CURRY
- 4 pounds very lean beef or lamb, all fat and gristle removed, cut into 1½-inch pieces
- ¼ cup salad oil
- 6 whole cloves, crushed, or ¾ teaspoon ground cloves
- ¾-inch piece of cinnamon, finely crushed
- Seeds from 5 whole cardamom pods, crushed
- 1 large onion, finely chopped

3 large tomatoes, peeled, seeded, and chopped, or 1½ cups canned
   plum tomatoes, drained and chopped
¼ cup grated unsweetened coconut, fresh or dried
8 dried apricots, coarsely chopped
3 hard pears, peeled, cored, and coarsely chopped
2 to 3 cups thin coconut milk
   Salt
   Tabasco or fresh minced chili pepper
   Juice of 1 lemon

Make sure that every speck of fat and gristle is removed from the
meat; the curry must not be greasy. Heat the oil in a heavy saucepan
large enough to hold all the ingredients. Add the cloves, cinnamon,
curry paste, and cardamom. Cook over medium heat, stirring constantly, for about 1 minute. Add the onion and cook, stirring constantly, until onion is soft. Add the meat and tomatoes. Cook,
stirring constantly, until the meat is browned, and the meat and tomatoes are covered with the spices. Add the coconut, apricots,
pears, and 2 cups of the coconut milk. Mix well. Season with salt
and Tabasco to taste. Bring to a boil. Reduce the heat to very low,
and simmer, covered, for 35 to 45 minutes, or until the meat is
tender but not mushy, stirring frequently. If too thick and in danger
of scorching, add a little more coconut milk, ¼ cup at a time. Remove from heat and stir in the lemon juice just before serving.

SHRIMP AND ARTICHOKE CURRY

Serves 4 to 6

1 pound small or medium shrimp
2 large artichokes
1 tablespoon butter
1 tablespoon olive oil
1 medium onion, thinly sliced
¼ cup chopped parsley
1½ teaspoons curry powder, or to taste
3 medium tomatoes, peeled and chopped
1 cup hot water or chicken bouillon
  Salt
  Juice of ½ lemon

Shell and devein the shrimp. Slice the artichokes according to directions on page 94. Heat the butter and olive oil together in a deep skillet or casserole. Add the onion and parsley. Cook over medium heat, stirring constantly, until onion is soft and golden. Add the curry powder. Cook, stirring constantly, for 3 minutes. Add the artichokes, tomatoes, and hot water. Simmer, covered, over low heat for 10 to 15 minutes, or until artichokes are three-quarters cooked. Add shrimp. Simmer, covered, for 5 to 7 minutes, or until shrimp are pink and artichokes are tender. Remove from heat, and stir in salt to taste and the lemon juice.

CURRIED LOBSTER OR SHRIMP SALAD

Cognac and mayonnaise are a happy combination.

Serves 4

3 cups cooked lobster, cut into bite-size pieces, or cooked and shelled shrimp (if shrimp are very large, cut into pieces)
1 9- or 10-ounce package frozen artichoke hearts, cooked, drained, and cut into thick slices
1 cup finely diced celery stalks, white part only
1 to 1⅓ cups mayonnaise
¼ cup Cognac or brandy
2 teaspoons curry powder
Salt
Dash Tabasco
Freshly ground pepper (optional)
Salad greens
Tomato wedges or red radishes

Combine the lobster or shrimp, artichoke hearts, and celery, and mix well. Combine the mayonnaise with the Cognac, curry powder, salt and Tabasco, and blend thoroughly. Add to the lobster or shrimp mixture and toss. Check the seasoning, and if necessary, add more salt and a little pepper. Put the salad greens into a serving dish or salad bowl and pile the salad on it. Garnish with tomato wedges or radishes.

Vegetables

The most depressing thing ever said about vegetables is that they are good for one, as if the human race ever abided by the reasonable dictum that one should do, or in this case eat, what is good for the human frame.

Unless properly cooked—that is, in as little water as possible, and only just enough to take away rawness but preserve crispness—vegetables can be most depressing. On the other hand, vegetables intended as an entity in themselves, and not merely as an accompaniment to worthier foods, are delicious. The French do this, and properly serve their vegetables as a separate course, a practice I think admirable, since in themselves vegetables do not really complement meats or fish, though habit decrees that this is so. There are only three simple rules for vegetable cookery, and here they come:

(1) The freshest vegetables are always the best; young and small ones are better than the larger and older; wilted and bruised vegetables are worthless.

(2) Vegetables should be cooked in a minimum of time and water.

(3) The water in which vegetables are cooked should be saved for soups and gravies.

FLEMISH ASPARAGUS WITH EGG SAUCE

This may be a luncheon main dish, followed by salad, cheese, and fruit. Allow 1 pound of asparagus for each serving.

Serves 4

4 hard-boiled eggs, mashed
1 cup butter, melted
Salt
Freshly ground pepper
2 tablespoons fresh lemon juice
2 tablespoons minced parsley
4 pounds asparagus, trimmed and peeled

In a small saucepan, combine the mashed eggs with the butter, and add salt and pepper to taste. Cook over low heat long enough to heat through thoroughly. Remove from heat and stir in the lemon juice and parsley; keep hot while the asparagus are cooking. Turn into a sauce dish and serve as soon as the asparagus are ready. Cook and drain the asparagus, and place the spears side by side on a clean kitchen towel. Line a serving platter with a large napkin folded in half. Place the asparagus on the lower part of the napkin and cover with the top half. This will absorb any moisture remaining in the asparagus.

STRING BEANS WITH CHEESE

Serves 3 or 4

1 pound string beans
3 tablespoons butter
⅔ cup grated Swiss cheese
Salt
Freshly ground pepper

Cook the beans in boiling salted water to cover until just tender but still crisp. Drain. Heat the butter in a stove-to-table skillet, but do not brown. Add beans and cook over medium heat, stirring constantly, for about 3 minutes. Sprinkle the cheese, and salt and pepper to taste, over beans and mix well. In a moment, there will be a golden crust at the bottom of the skillet, and the dish is ready to serve.

ROMAN FAVA OR BROAD BEANS

*Pancetta, pork cured in salt and spices and found in Italian
food stores, is used as a flavoring in Rome in the way we use
bacon. It has a definite, pleasing flavor. When none is available, use prosciutto or bacon, though the flavor of the dish
will be different. Serve with roast pork or lamb.*

Serves 4

    4 pounds fava beans in the pod
    1 tablespoon lard or olive oil
    1 small onion, minced
    ¼ pound pancetta or bacon, cut into ¼-inch strips
    ¼ cup water or beef bouillon
      Salt
      Freshly ground pepper

Shell the fava beans. If they are very large, remove the tough skin
with the tip of a sharp knife. Heat the lard in a heavy saucepan.
Sauté the onion until golden. Add the pancetta and cook for 1 minute longer. Add the fava beans, water, and salt and pepper to taste.
Mix well. Simmer, covered, over low heat for 5 to 15 minutes, depending on the size and toughness of the beans. Stir frequently and
check the moisture and seasoning.

BEANS WITH SAGE

Good with pork or lamb.

Serves 4 to 6

1½ cups dried white beans, soaked and ready to cook
 2 tablespoons butter
 3 tablespoons olive oil
 2 to 3 tablespoons minced fresh sage leaves, or 1 to 1½ teaspoons dried sage
   Salt
   Freshly ground pepper
 ⅓ cup any fresh tomato sauce, or drained chopped tomatoes

Cook the beans in boiling water to cover plus 3 inches for 45 minutes to 1 hour, or until beans are tender. This must be done over very low heat to prevent the beans from bursting open. Do not add salt or the beans will be tough. Drain. Heat together the butter and olive oil. Add beans, sage, and salt and pepper to taste. Cook over medium heat for about 3 minutes, stirring with a fork so as not to break the beans. Add the tomato sauce and cook for 3 minutes longer, or until sauce and beans are very hot.

MEXICAN BEANPOT

Serve as a lunch or supper main dish with a tossed salad.

Serves 6 to 8

2 pounds black beans
3 quarts water
1 large onion
1 clove garlic
1 bay leaf
1 tablespoon bacon fat, lard, or salad oil
1 pound cooked ham (preferably smoked ham), ground
1 cup tomato juice
  Salt
  Freshly ground pepper
1 teaspoon ground cumin (optional)
1 teaspoon dried marjoram
1 pound cooked ham (preferably smoked ham), trimmed of fat
  and cut into 1-inch cubes
  Sour cream

Wash the beans and pick them over. Soak them overnight in the water. The next day, add the onion, garlic, and bay leaf. Bring to a boil, then reduce the heat. Cover and simmer for 2 hours. Remove onion, garlic, and bay leaf. Heat the bacon fat in a skillet. Cook the ground ham for about 2 to 3 minutes. Stirring constantly, add the tomato juice, salt and pepper to taste, the cumin, and the marjoram. Stir ham mixture into beans. Simmer, covered, for 30 minutes longer. Add the ham cubes and simmer for 10 minutes longer. Top each serving with a spoonful of sour cream.

SUGAR-BROWNED CARROTS

A standard Danish recipe.

Serves 4

4 large or 6 medium carrots, cut into thin 3- or 4-inch strips
3 tablespoons butter
2 tablespoons sugar
  Salt

Wash and drain the carrots. Put carrots into a saucepan and add just enough boiling water to barely cover. Cook, covered, for 3 to 4 minutes or until just tender; carrots must remain crisp. Drain and keep warm in a heated dish. Heat the butter in a frying pan. Stir in the sugar. Cook over low heat, stirring constantly, until the sugar has melted and is golden. Add carrots. Cook, stirring constantly with a fork, until the carrots are golden on all sides. Do not scorch. Sprinkle with salt to taste. Serve very hot.

SPANISH SAUTÉED CHICKPEAS

GARBANZOS FRITOS

Chickpeas, which look like little yellow bullets, are eaten out of hand, put in soups, in stews, and combined with meats. Chickpeas come dried and can be prepared like any other dried bean—that is, soaked in water, then boiled in salted water until soft. Or they can be bought canned. When using canned chickpeas, wash off their liquid under cold-running water and drain well. Chickpeas ought to be better known as a substitute for the eternal potatoes. The following recipe goes well with fish, which the nutlike flavor of the chickpeas seems to complement.

Serves 4

¼ cup olive oil
2 cups cooked chickpeas
  Salt
  Freshly ground pepper
⅓ cup chopped parsley

Heat olive oil in a saucepan. Cook the chickpeas lightly until heated through. Season with salt and pepper to taste, and sprinkle with parsley. Serve as you would potatoes.

TANTE MARIE'S MUSHROOMS SAUTÉED WITH HERBS

Serves 2 as main dish;
4 as appetizer (about 2 cups)

1 clove garlic, cut in half
¼ cup butter
4 slices firm-type white bread, crusts removed
1 pound mushrooms, whole if small, quartered if medium, cut into eighths if large
2 tablespoons minced parsley
1 tablespoon minced chives
  Salt
  Freshly ground pepper
4 lemon wedges

Rub a frying pan large enough to hold the bread slices in a single layer with the garlic. Discard garlic. Add 2 tablespoons of the butter to frying pan and brown slightly. Add bread slices. Brown bread on both sides over low heat, turning once. Remove bread to a heated serving dish and keep warm. Add the remaining 2 tablespoons butter to pan and brown slightly. Cook the mushrooms quickly over medium to high heat until just tender, about 3 minutes, stirring frequently. Do not overcook mushrooms; if mushrooms are overcooked, they may exude their juices and become rubbery in texture. Stir in the parsley and chives. Season with salt and pepper to taste. Spoon mushrooms over bread. Squeeze 1 lemon wedge over each serving. Serve at once.

Onions à la Grecque

Serves 6

36 small white onions (the smaller, the better), peeled
⅔ cup olive oil
2 cups dry white wine
1 cup water
½ cup white vinegar
2 tablespoons tomato paste
2 cloves garlic, mashed
2 whole cloves
1 teaspoon each of dried tarragon, crumbled, salt, coarsely ground pepper, dry mustard, and mustard seed
½ cup golden raisins
½ cup minced parsley

Combine all the ingredients except the raisins and parsley in a large deep frying pan. Bring to a boil. Reduce the heat to very low and simmer, covered, for 10 minutes. Add the raisins and simmer for about 5 more minutes, or until the onions are tender but still hold their shape; exact cooking time will depend on their size. Cool and let stand at room temperature for 2 hours, then chill. Sprinkle with the parsley before serving with hot or cold roast meats.

SHERRIED ONIONS

Serves 4 or 5

18 small white onions, peeled
 1 teaspoon salt
 ¼ cup butter
 ½ teaspoon sugar
   Freshly ground pepper
 ⅓ cup medium-dry sherry
 ¼ cup minced parsley

Place the onions in a saucepan and add enough boiling water to come up to 1 inch on the sides of the pan. Add the salt. Bring to a boil and cook without a cover for 5 minutes. Cover and cook for about 10 minutes, or until the onions are just tender. Pour off any water that remains. Add the butter, sugar, pepper to taste, and the sherry. Cook over medium heat for about 3 to 4 minutes. Turn into a serving dish and sprinkle with the parsley. Serve with roast meats.

Lemon Potatoes

Serves 4 to 6

2 pounds small new potatoes or 2 pounds all-purpose potatoes
¼ cup olive oil
2 tablespoons fresh lemon juice
  Grated rind of ½ lemon
  Salt
  Freshly ground pepper
1 teaspoon dried oregano (optional)

If the potatoes are small and new, scrub but do not peel them. If using all-purpose potatoes, peel and cut into 2-inch pieces. Cook the potatoes in plenty of boiling salted water until barely tender; they must not overcook or they will be watery. Drain and return to the saucepan. Over moderate heat, shake the saucepan with the potatoes to dry them out completely. Turn into a heated serving dish and keep warm. While the potatoes are cooking, combine the remaining ingredients and beat until creamy. Pour over the potatoes, toss with two forks, and serve warm, lukewarm, or chilled.

SWISS FRIED POTATO CAKE

ROESTI

*A famous Swiss recipe and a change from home-fried pota-
toes. Since the potatoes should be thoroughly cooled and
firm, they should be cooked well ahead of time; a day ahead is
best.*

Serves 4

2 pounds potatoes
4 to 6 tablespoons butter
   Salt
   Freshly ground pepper
2 to 4 tablespoons hot water

Cook the potatoes in their skins in boiling salted water and cool
thoroughly at room temperature. Peel and shred on a shredder or
cut into small julienne strips. Heat 4 tablespoons of the butter in a
heavy frying pan. Add potatoes and season with salt and pepper to
taste. Cook over low heat, turning frequently to coat the potatoes
with the butter, until they are soft and yellow. Add the remaining
butter to the frying pan. Press the potatoes with the spatula into a
flat cake. Sprinkle with 2 tablespoons of the hot water. Cover and
cook over low heat for about 15 to 20 minutes, or until potatoes are
golden and crusty at the bottom. Shake the pan frequently to prevent sticking. Check for moisture; if potatoes look very dry, sprinkle
with the remaining water. Turn into a heated serving dish crusty
side up and serve immediately.

    VARIATION
Add ½ cup diced Swiss cheese to the potatoes before cooking and
mix well.

POTATO AND CHEESE TART

Serves 4

3 medium potatoes, boiled, peeled, and mashed
1 cup flour
Salt
Freshly ground pepper
½ cup olive oil
1 cup drained canned tomatoes
½ pound mozzarella cheese, cut into ½-inch cubes
¼ cup freshly grated Parmesan cheese
1 tablespoon dried rosemary, crumbled

Preheat the oven to hot (400° F).

Mix together the potatoes, flour, and salt and pepper to taste to make a smooth paste. (Using your hands is the easiest way.) Generously grease a 9-inch flat baking dish. Line the bottom with the potato mixture, making a layer ¼ to ½ inch thick. Sprinkle with ¼ cup of the olive oil. Top with the tomatoes, the mozarella and Parmesan cheeses, and sprinkle with the rosemary and remaining ¼ cup olive oil. Bake for 20 minutes, or until browned. Serve hot as a first course or as a side dish with cold meats.

CRUSTLESS POTHERB PIE

There is a certain amount of waste in leafy greens, such as wilted leaves, tough stems, etc. To come out with the wanted amount of trimmed greens, buy ½ to 1 pound more, depending on their condition. The amount below makes about 3 cups cooked greens that have been squeezed very dry and chopped. Like all greens, uncooked they will fill the kettle to overflowing but will cook down a great deal.

Serves 6

2 pounds Swiss chard, trimmed
2 pounds spinach, trimmed
1 pound dandelion greens, trimmed
3 tablespoons bacon fat
¼ cup butter
2 cloves garlic, minced
½ cup pine nuts
3 eggs, lightly beaten
1 cup light cream or milk
1 cup freshly grated Parmesan cheese
½ teaspoon ground nutmeg
  Salt
  Freshly ground pepper
⅓ cup currants or seedless raisins, plumped in warm water and drained
  About ⅓ cup fine dry bread crumbs

Preheat the oven to moderate (350° F).

Wash the greens in at least 3 changes of cold water, or until not a trace of sand or dirt remains in the water. Drain but do not shake dry. Put the greens into a large kettle with the water that clings to the leaves. Cook, covered, over high heat for about 8 to 10 minutes, or until tender. Do not overcook the greens or they will lose their flavor. Drain in a colander over a bowl; save the cooking liquid for soups, stews, or sauces—it is full of vitamins. First with the back of a wooden spoon and then with the hands, squeeze as much water as possible out of the greens. Put them on a chopping board and chop medium fine. Drain the chopped greens again, squeezing with the hands. Put the greens into a large bowl.

Heat the bacon fat and 2 tablespoons of the butter in a large deep frying pan. Cook the garlic and pine nuts over medium heat, stirring constantly, until the pine nuts are golden. Add the chopped greens. Cook, stirring constantly, for about 7 to 10 minutes, or until the greens are thoroughly coated with the fat. Return the cooked greens to the bowl. Beat together the eggs, cream, ⅔ cup of the cheese, and the nutmeg. Check the seasoning (the cheese is salty) and add salt and pepper to taste. Stir in the currants. Pour this mixture over the greens and mix well. Butter a 10-inch shallow baking dish or pie plate and coat it with bread crumbs. Turn the vegetable mixture into dish and smooth out the top. Sprinkle with the remaining ⅓ cup cheese and dot with the remaining 2 tablespoons butter. Bake for 10 minutes, then reduce the heat to 325° F and bake for 20 to 30 minutes, or until set and browned. Cut into wedges and serve warm or cool but not chilled.

SPINACH SOUFFLÉ

Serves 4

3 tablespoons butter
¼ cup flour
 Salt
 Freshly ground pepper
⅛ teaspoon ground nutmeg
1 cup light cream or milk
1 cup grated Swiss or Parmesan cheese
1 cup finely chopped cooked spinach, well drained and with as
  much liquid squeezed out as possible
3 eggs, separated

Preheat the oven to slow (325° F).

Melt the butter and blend in the flour, salt and pepper to taste, and the nutmeg. Gradually add the cream, stirring until well blended. Cook over low heat, stirring constantly, until thick and smooth. Add the cheese and spinach, and cook until cheese is melted. Cool. Beat the egg yolks until thick. Add to spinach mixture. Beat egg whites until stiff but not dry and fold into spinach. Pour into a buttered 1½-quart baking dish and bake for about 45 to 50 minutes.

SPINACH TIMBALES

Serves 6

1 10-ounce package frozen chopped spinach
2 tablespoons butter
¼ pound mushrooms, sliced (about 1⅓ cups)
1 tablespoon flour
¼ cup heavy cream
¼ teaspoon salt, or to taste
¼ teaspoon freshly ground pepper
1 10-ounce package frozen patty shells, thawed
2 tablespoons fine dry bread crumbs
1 egg, beaten

Preheat the oven to moderate (350° F).

Place the frozen spinach in a large saucepan. Cover and cook over low heat until spinach is tender, 10 to 20 minutes, turning spinach occasionally until thawed, then stirring occasionally while cooking. Drain in strainer. Press spinach firmly against sides of strainer with spoon to thoroughly drain spinach of all water; reserve. You should have ¾ cup spinach.

Melt the butter in the same saucepan. Cook the mushrooms quickly over medium to high heat until barely tender, about 2 to 3 minutes, stirring frequently. Reduce the heat to low. Stir in the flour. Cook for 1 to 2 minutes, stirring constantly. Stir in the cream. Cook, stirring constantly, until mixture thickens. Stir in the spinach, salt, and pepper. Heat just until hot; set aside.

For each timbale, cut off approximately one third of patty shell pastry and set aside for top. Roll remaining patty shell pastry into a 5-inch circle. Line a 3¼x1½x1¼-inch ungreased tart pan with pastry circle. Sprinkle top and sides with ½ teaspoon bread crumbs. Spoon in a scant ¼ cup spinach filling. Sprinkle on ½ teaspoon bread crumbs. Roll reserved patty shell dough into a 3-inch circle. Place on top of filling. Using fingers, tightly seal top edge of pastry to bottom edge, completely enclosing spinach filling. Shape edge to shape of tart pan. Repeat procedure, making 5 additional timbales. Lightly brush top and edges with some of the egg. Place tart pans on a baking sheet. Bake for 30 to 35 minutes, or until golden brown. Run a sharp knife around edges and carefully lift out timbales. Serve warm. To reheat, place in low oven (250° to 300° F) and heat just until hot.

NOTE: Six 6-ounce custard cups may be substituted for fluted tart pans. When lining custard cups with 5-inch circle of pastry, line only to ½ inch from top, then proceed as above. Flute edges using fork.

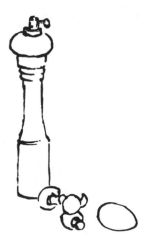

BAKED TOMATOES

A recipe from the Eastern Shore of Maryland, as given to me by a now defunct lady of St. Michael, quoted here verbatim.

Serves 5 or 6

2 2-pound cans tomatoes, drained and chopped
1 cup sugar
1 teaspoon salt
¼ cup cornstarch
¼ cup butter
⅓ cup medium-dry sherry
  Freshly ground pepper (optional)
1 to 2 teaspoons fresh lemon juice

Preheat the oven to moderate (375° F).

In a saucepan, combine the tomatoes, sugar, salt, cornstarch, butter, and sherry. Cook, stirring frequently, until the mixture is thick. Season with pepper if desired. Transfer the tomatoes to a buttered baking dish. Bake for about 20 minutes, or until the tomatoes are golden brown on the top and darker brown on the sides. Stir in the lemon juice and serve as a vegetable side dish with meat.

ROMAN STUFFED TOMATOES

*On the display tables of Roman restaurants, when the big to-
matoes that we call beefsteak tomatoes are in season, one sees
large pans of them stuffed with rice. The dish is an unusually
good one, and rather unknown outside of Rome. It can be
eaten either hot or cold.*

*It is difficult to give an accurate amount for the uncooked
rice that is used to stuff the tomatoes, since the size of tomatoes varies so. Roughly speaking, about 2 tablespoons are
needed if the tomatoes are large. If any rice stuffing is left
over, bake it alongside the tomatoes in the pan.*

Serves 6

8 medium to large tomatoes
½ cup olive oil
⅓ cup chopped parsley
2 cloves garlic, minced
1 cup rice
2 cups hot chicken bouillon
Salt
Freshly ground pepper
⅛ teaspoon ground cinnamon (optional)

Preheat the oven to moderate (350° F).

Cut a slice from the top of each tomato, then scoop out tomatoes
with a spoon without breaking the walls. Strain and save the juice.
Place tomatoes in a shallow baking dish. Sprinkle each tomato with
a little olive oil—use 2 to 3 tablespoons. Heat the remaining oil in a
heavy saucepan. Add the parsley and garlic and sauté over medium
heat for 3 minutes. Add the rice and cook for 3 minutes longer, stirring constantly. Add the chicken bouillon. Cover and cook for 10
minutes, or until rice is three-quarters done; cooking time will vary
depending on the kind of rice used. Remove from heat. Add salt and
pepper to taste, and cinnamon. Fill tomatoes with rice mixture. Pour
the reserved tomato juice over tomatoes to a depth of ½ inch. Bake
for 30 to 40 minutes, or until rice is tender and liquid is absorbed. If
during baking time the tomatoes show signs of drying out, add a little hot water. Baste occasionally.

CURRIED TURNIPS

Also try with parsnips. Serve with ham.

Serves 4 to 6

3 tablespoons butter
1 medium onion, minced
1 tablespoon curry powder, or to taste
½ to 1 cup hot chicken bouillon or water
2 pounds turnips, peeled and cut into 1-inch cubes
Salt
Freshly ground pepper
½ cup plain yogurt

Heat the butter in a heavy saucepan. Sauté the onion until soft. Stir in the curry powder. Cook, stirring constantly, for 2 to 3 minutes. Stir in ½ cup of the bouillon. Add the turnips. Cook, covered, over very low heat for about 10 to 15 minutes, or until turnips are tender. Check the moisture; if necessary to prevent scorching, add more bouillon, 2 tablespoons at a time. The cooked turnips should be dry. Season with salt and pepper to taste. Remove from heat and stir in the yogurt. Serve immediately.

BAKED ZUCCHINI AND RICE

TIAN DE COURGETTES

This dish may serve as a first course, preferably with a tomato or mushroom sauce. As an accompaniment to meat, it will serve as a starch/vegetable in one. I think it is better to drain the zucchini after sautéeing in order to get a firmer dish.

Serves 6

⅓ cup long-grain rice
2 pounds zucchini
1 tablespoon salt
¼ cup olive oil
1 small onion, minced
2 eggs, beaten
⅔ cup grated or shredded Swiss cheese
⅓ cup minced parsley
1 teaspoon dried thyme or basil (optional)
  Salt
  Freshly ground pepper
2 tablespoons fresh bread crumbs or 1 to 2 tomatoes, sliced

Cook the rice in plenty of boiling water until it is soft but not mushy; drain and reserve. Trim the zucchini and shred it on a grater or in a food processor. Place shredded zucchini in a colander and sprinkle with the salt. Mix well and place over a bowl or in the sink. Let stand for 15 to 30 minutes. Drain well and squeeze dry with the sides of a spoon or with your hands.

Preheat the oven to moderate (350° F).

Lightly grease a shallow 8 x 10-inch baking dish that can go to the table. Heat 3 tablespoons of the olive oil in a large frying pan. Cook the onion and zucchini over low heat, stirring frequently, for 5 to 10 minutes, or until mixture turns golden. (This step adds flavor to the finished dish.) Turn zucchini and rice into a large bowl. Add the eggs, cheese, and parsley, the thyme if desired, and add pepper to taste. Mix well. Check the seasoning; if necessary, add salt to taste.

Turn into baking dish and smooth out top. Sprinkle with the bread crumbs or top with tomato slices. Drizzle with the remaining tablespoon olive oil. Bake for about 25 minutes, or until top is golden and firm. Serve hot or lukewarm.

MARINATED ZUCCHINI

This is a dish from Giannino, one of Milan's finest restaurants. It can also be made with yellow squash, or even eggplant, and will keep for at least 3 days in the refrigerator. Serve well chilled.

Serves 4 to 6

6 zucchini
  Olive oil for sautéeing
1 cup mild vinegar
½ cup olive oil
½ teaspoon minced garlic
6 chopped fresh basil leaves or 1 tablespoon dried basil
  Salt
  Freshly ground pepper
2 tablespoons chopped parsley

Trim the zucchini, scrape lightly (to remove waxy coating), and cut into 1½-inch sticks—the size of a little finger. Sauté in olive oil until golden. Drain on paper towels. Combine the vinegar, olive oil, garlic, basil, and salt and pepper to taste, and simmer for 5 minutes. Arrange zucchini in layers in a glass or china dish; do not use metal. Pour hot marinade over zucchini and sprinkle with parsley. Cover and chill at least overnight. Drain before serving with roast or grilled meats or poultry.

NOTE: Do not oversauté the zucchini; they should have body and not be mushy.

RATATOUILLE

This is the vegetable stew of Provence, to be eaten hot or cold. The vegetables should be simmered in the oil, not fried. The ingredients listed below are the classic ones, but I sometimes add, with good effect, a handful of sliced okra, and even a little fresh cut corn from the cob.

Serves 4 to 6

1 medium eggplant
   Salt
½ cup olive oil
2 large onions, sliced
1 clove garlic, minced
2 sweet peppers, red or green, diced
4 large tomatoes, peeled and chopped
2 zucchini, sliced
   Freshly ground pepper
2 tablespoons chopped parsley
¼ teaspoon dried marjoram
¼ teaspoon dried basil or thyme

Peel the eggplant and cut into ½-inch thick slices. To drain off the excess liquid in the eggplant, salt the slices lightly and place in a colander. Place a plate on top of the eggplant, weigh down with a heavy can or two, and allow to drain for 30 minutes to 1 hour.

Cut eggplant slices into 1½-inch pieces. Heat the olive oil in a large skillet over low heat. The oil must not be very hot. Cook—but do not fry—the onions, garlic, and peppers until soft. Add the tomatoes, zucchini, and eggplant. Season with salt and pepper to taste, and add the parsley, marjoram, and basil. Simmer, covered, over low heat for about 30 minutes. Uncover and simmer for 10 minutes longer, or until liquid is absorbed.

Sauces and Relishes

Basically, people fall into two categories: those who like wet food and those who like dry food. I belong to the latter; as my husband says, I am a natural patron to the Dust and Ashes Restaurant and the Dead Sea Bakery. I would also like to add that Italian food, on which I was brought up, is never heavily sauced; we are a dry food nation. This may be neither here nor there, but it explains the scarcity of sauces in this book on the principle that those who like sauces and gravies will know where to find good recipes. (Standard cookbooks such as *The Doubleday Cookbook* [1975] by Jean Anderson are a great help.) But if you do make sauces, remember that reducing and reducing and reducing again is the secret of a good flavorful sauce. Be careful when putting in the salt; reducing makes a sauce salty in itself.

Even though I don't care for sauces, I like relishes because they cheer up ordinary foods and also because they are fun to make. They give you a lasting result for your cooking efforts, and besides, relishes add kudos to the cook's reputation. When making relishes at home, remember to cook them in an enamelware, glass, or stainless steel vessel that will not discolor the food or affect its taste, and to stir the preparation almost constantly to prevent burning.

BETTY'S THICK BERNAISE SAUCE

Not as acid as the classic recipe, and surprisingly pleasant on plain linguine or other thin pasta.

About 1⅓ cups

½ cup sweet butter
¼ cup dry white wine
2 tablespoons wine vinegar
4 tablespoons minced fresh tarragon or 2 teaspoons dried tarragon
½ teaspoon salt
Freshly ground pepper
6 large egg yolks

Melt the butter in a small saucepan (do not use aluminum) or in top of a double boiler. Meanwhile, in a small bowl, whisk together the wine, vinegar, tarragon, salt, pepper to taste, and egg yolks. Pour the egg yolk mixture into the melted butter. Whisk mixture constantly over low heat or over simmering water until mixture begins to thicken. Remove from heat immediately. (Sauce will continue to thicken after it is removed from heat.) Set saucepan in pan of cold water for 1 minute to prevent further cooking, whisking constantly. Spoon into a heated serving bowl.

MADEIRA AND JUNIPER BERRY SAUCE

This sauce goes well with pâté, ham, or game birds.

About 1⅓ cups

2 tablespoons butter
2 tablespoons flour
1 cup beef bouillon
½ cup Madeira
  Salt
  Freshly ground pepper
1 to 2 teaspoons ground juniper berries (see Note)

Heat the butter until brown. Stir in the flour and cook over low heat for 5 minutes, stirring constantly. The mixture should be medium brown. Add the bouillon and simmer for 15 to 20 minutes, stirring occasionally. Add the Madeira, salt and pepper to taste, and the ground juniper berries. Simmer for another 10 minutes. If the sauce is too thick, dilute with a little more bouillon, one tablespoon at a time.

NOTE: Juniper berries can be ground in a nut grinder, pounded in a mortar, or put between two sheets of wax paper and crushed with a rolling pin.

ENGLISH BREAD SAUCE

For roast chicken, turkey, and other birds, especially when they are not stuffed.

About 1⅔ cups

1 medium onion stuck with 3 whole cloves
1 bay leaf
2 cups milk
3 to 4 tablespoons fresh white bread crumbs (made without crusts)
  Salt
  Freshly ground pepper
⅛ teaspoon ground nutmeg or ½ teaspoon cayenne pepper (both ingredients and quantities are optional)
1 tablespoon butter
1 tablespoon heavy cream

Put the onion, bay leaf, and milk into a saucepan. Cover and barely simmer over very low heat for 15 to 20 minutes, or until the milk is well flavored. Remove onion and bay leaf, and stir the bread crumbs into milk. Simmer over low heat for about 5 minutes, or until sauce is thickened and creamy, stirring constantly. Remove from heat and season with salt and pepper to taste, and the nutmeg. Blend in the butter and cream. Reheat gently and serve at once.

NOTE: Depending on individual preference, this sauce can be made thicker or thinner. If a thicker sauce is wanted, add 1 to 2 more tablespoons bread crumbs. If a thinner sauce is called for, decrease the bread crumbs accordingly. The main thing is to have a sauce that is well flavored with onion and seasonings.

BRANDIED CRANBERRY SAUCE

For puddings or as an ice cream topping.

About 1¾ cups

1½ cups whole cranberry sauce
⅓ cup brandy
2 teaspoons cornstarch

Blend together all the ingredients in a saucepan. Cook, stirring constantly until the sauce is glossy and thickened. Serve warm or chilled.

ENGLISH CUMBERLAND SAUCE

An excellent sauce, named after the Duke of Cumberland,
King of Hanover. Serve it cold with either hot or cold meat.

About 1¾ to 2 cups

1 cup red currant jelly
1 cup port
  Juice of ½ lemon
  Juice of ½ orange
2 teaspoons grated lemon rind
2 teaspoons grated orange rind
2 teaspoons dry English mustard
  Salt
  Freshly ground pepper
¼ teaspoon cayenne pepper
¼ teaspoon ground ginger

Melt the currant jelly. Stir in the port and lemon and orange juice; cool. Blend in all the other ingredients.

GREEK GARLIC SAUCE

SKORDALIA

This very popular Greek sauce is wonderful with fish and vegetables.

About 2½ cups

6 medium potatoes
4 to 6 cloves garlic, minced
1 teaspoon salt
¾ to 1 cup olive oil
¼ cup fresh lemon juice

Boil the potatoes in their skins. In a mortar, pound the garlic and salt to a smooth paste. Or blend in a blender or food processor. Peel potatoes and, while hot, add them to the garlic mixture, blending everything to a smooth paste. Gradually add the olive oil, a few drops at a time, alternating with the lemon juice. The sauce should be very smooth and the consistency of thick cream.

NOTE: The amount of olive oil may have to be adjusted, since different kinds of potatoes absorb olive oil differently. Mealy potatoes are best for this sauce.

MORNAY SAUCE

A rich cheese sauce for eggs, fish, vegetables, and white meats. It can be made with any kind of cooking cheese, but I think that a mixture of Parmesan and Swiss gives the best flavor.

About 1⅔ cups

3 tablespoons butter
3 tablespoons flour
½ teaspoon salt
¼ teaspoon ground white pepper
¾ cup hot chicken bouillon
¾ cup hot light or heavy cream
1 small onion stuck with 1 whole clove
½ cup freshly grated Parmesan cheese
½ cup grated Swiss cheese

Melt the butter and remove from heat. Blend in the flour, salt, and pepper. Cook over low heat, stirring constantly, for 1 to 2 minutes; do not brown. Gradually add the hot bouillon and cream, stirring constantly until smooth. Add the onion. Cook over low heat, stirring constantly, until thick and very smooth. Continue cooking 5 minutes longer. Remove onion. Add the Parmesan and Swiss cheeses and stir until well blended.

MUSHROOM SPAGHETTI SAUCE

About 3½ cups

6 tablespoons butter
4 medium onions, thinly sliced
2 pounds mushrooms, sliced
  Salt
  Freshly ground pepper
¼ teaspoon ground nutmeg
1 cup heavy cream

Heat 3 tablespoons of the butter in a heavy frying pan. Sauté the onions over medium heat for 5 to 7 minutes, or until golden brown, stirring frequently. Cover and cook onions over very low heat for 20 minutes, or until very soft, stirring occasionally. Melt the remaining 3 tablespoons butter in another frying pan and cook the mushrooms until tender. Season with salt and pepper to taste, and add the nutmeg. Add mushrooms to onions. Keep sauce hot while spaghetti is cooking according to package directions. Five minutes before serving, add the cream to sauce and heat thoroughly. Do not let boil or the sauce will curdle. Mix cooked spaghetti and sauce thoroughly, and serve immediately with grated Parmesan cheese.

PIZZAIOLA TOMATO SAUCE

The tomatoes should cook just long enough to soften, or the sauce will lose its very fresh taste. Pizzaiola sauce is usually served on steaks, but it is excellent on the lighter pasta varieties, such as spaghetti, linguine, or thin noodles.

About 3 to 3½ cups

¼ cup olive oil
1½ to 2 pounds fresh tomatoes, peeled, seeded, and chopped
2 cloves garlic, minced
Salt
Freshly ground pepper
1 teaspoon dried oregano, 1 tablespoon chopped fresh basil leaves, or 2 tablespoons chopped parsley

Heat the olive oil in a heavy saucepan. Add the tomatoes, garlic, salt and pepper to taste, and the oregano. Cook over high heat for about 10 minutes, or until tomatoes are just soft.

ENGLISH GOOSEBERRY SAUCE

Gooseberries are used a great deal in England and in northern Europe for desserts and preserves. The English also make this excellent sauce from gooseberries, and it goes extremely well with boiled or fried fish and other fried foods, as well as with rich fowl, such as duck or goose. Gooseberries turn up quite frequently in American markets, but unless people are of European descent, they don't know what to make of them. Since American gooseberries are much more acid than their European cousins, this sauce is a good way of utilizing them.

About 1¾ cups

1 pint gooseberries
1 cup water
  Handful of spinach or sorrel leaves, chopped (optional, see Note)
1 tablespoon butter
⅛ teaspoon ground nutmeg
  Sugar

Cook the gooseberries and water together until berries are soft. Add the spinach leaves and cook for 3 minutes longer. Drain and reserve juice. Rub berries and spinach through a food mill or a fine sieve. (A food processor would make the juice a little grainy, which I don't like.) Return purée to saucepan and combine with juice. The purée should be the consistency of a thin batter; if too liquid, boil over high heat until right consistency is achieved by evaporation. Add the butter and nutmeg, and sugar to taste. Simmer for 2 to 3 minutes, stirring constantly.

NOTE: If no spinach is used, add a few drops of green food coloring to obtain the right color.

CAUCASIAN PLUM SAUCE

TKEMALI

Very good for roast chicken or other roast fowl and for shashlik.

About 1½ cups

½ pound blue plums, pitted
2 to 3 cloves garlic, minced
1 tablespoon minced parsley
Salt
Freshly ground pepper
Tabasco

Cook the plums in water to cover. Drain and reserve liquid. Rub plums through a sieve, or purée in a blender or food processor. Stir sufficient plum liquid into the purée to achieve the consistency of heavy cream. Add the garlic and parsley, and season with salt, pepper, and Tabasco to taste. Bring to a boil, then reduce the heat and simmer for 5 minutes.

REMOULADE SAUCE

A piquant sauce much used in France, Germany, and the Scandinavian countries on fish and sea food, cold meats, and vegetable salads.

About 1½ cups

- 1 teaspoon dry English mustard
- 1 teaspoon paprika
- ¼ teaspoon salt
- ¼ teaspoon freshly ground pepper
- ¼ teaspoon cayenne pepper
- 2 teaspoons prepared horseradish
- 4 anchovy fillets, minced
- 1 tablespoon minced capers
- 2 tablespoons minced green onions
- 2 tablespoons minced celery
- 3 tablespoons wine vinegar
- ⅔ cup olive oil

Combine all the ingredients, and beat until thoroughly mixed and blended.

EASY SEAFOOD SAUCE

About 1½ cups

1 cup mayonnaise
2 tablespoons heavy cream
1 tablespoon ketchup
3 tablespoons Cognac or brandy

Combine all the ingredients and blend thoroughly. Chill before serving with shrimp, lobster, or crabmeat.

UNCOOKED PIQUANT GREEN SAUCE

A classic sauce of Italian cookery that is found in all regions with slight variations. This is the recipe of the great nineteenth-century cook Artusi, the dean of classic Italian cookery. A blender or food processor is ideal for this sauce, since it eliminates much tiresome chopping and mincing. The sauce is excellent for hot and cold boiled and broiled meats, seafood, hard-boiled eggs (as an antipasto), and cooked vegetables such as artichokes, cardoon, cauliflower, and broccoli.

About 1⅓ cups

2 tablespoons capers, drained
1 tablespoon minced onion
1 clove garlic, minced
2 anchovy fillets, chopped
2 cups tightly packed parsley heads (no stems)
1 teaspoon dried basil or minced fresh basil leaves to taste
¾ cup olive oil
 Juice of 2 lemons
1 teaspoon salt
¼ teaspoon freshly ground pepper

Combine all the ingredients in a blender or food processor. Blend to a purée. Or mince together to a pulp the capers, onion, garlic, and anchovy fillets. Mince together until very fine the parsley and basil. Combine with the caper mixture. Slowly beat in the oil, lemon juice, salt, and pepper. Blend thoroughly.

White Wine
Salad Dressing

To my mind, this dressing is far better for cooked vegetable, meat, and seafood salads than the ordinary French dressing.

About 1⅓ cups

¾ cup dry white wine
½ cup olive oil
¼ cup tarragon vinegar
¼ cup minced onion
½ clove garlic, minced (can be left out or increased to taste)
  Salt
  Freshly ground pepper

Combine all the ingredients and blend thoroughly. Use while foods to be dressed are still hot.

SPICED BANANA RELISH

Good with ham, pork, or poultry, hot or cold.

About 5 to 6 cups

- 2 cups sugar
- ¾ cup cider or white vinegar
- ¼ cup fresh lemon juice
- 2 tablespoons butter
- 3 2-inch pieces cinnamon
- 1½ teaspoons whole cloves
- 1 to 2 teaspoons minced fresh gingerroot or 2 teaspoons ground ginger (fresh ginger is preferable)
- ⅛ teaspoon salt (optional)
- ¼ teaspoon ground nutmeg
- ¼ teaspoon ground mace
- 4 large firm green bananas or firm unripe yellow bananas, peeled and cut into 1-inch rounds

Combine all the ingredients except the bananas in a saucepan large enough to hold the bananas. If possible, use an enameled or stainless steel saucepan, but it is not fatal to use an aluminum pan. Bring to a boil over medium heat. Reduce the heat to low and simmer for 3 minutes. Add bananas and simmer for 5 minutes; bananas must be tender but still firm. Cool bananas in the liquid. With a slotted spoon, transfer bananas to a serving dish. Scrape off the cinnamon and cloves.

NOTE: Strain the remaining liquid and use it for pork chops or ham as a cooking or basting liquid.

LEMON CHUTNEY

About 5 cups

4 lemons and 1 lime or 5 lemons
4 to 6 hot chili peppers, green or red
4 medium onions, minced
1 cup golden raisins
1 cup dark raisins
1 cup chopped prunes, apricots, or dates (or a combination)
1 pound sugar
1 tablespoon salt
1½ pints cider vinegar

Pare the zest—the yellow and green part of the rind—from the lemons and the lime, leaving the white pith. Chop it very fine and put into a blender. Squeeze the lemons and the lime, and add the juice to the zest in the blender. Wash and seed the chili peppers, and cut off the membranes. As soon as you have trimmed the chilis, wash them under cold running water, making sure that none of the seeds sticks—the seeds are *very* hot. Cut chilis into small pieces and add to the blender mixture. (Do not touch your eyes while you are working with the chilis because their oils will sting you badly. Wash your hands immediately and thoroughly with hot water and soap after you have finished with the chilis.) Whirl the blender until chilis, zest, and juice are amalgamated and smooth. In a bowl, combine the onions, raisins, prunes and sugar. Mix well. Pour the lemon-lime juice mixture over the onions and fruit and mix together. Let stand at room temperature for 2 to 3 hours; the time does not matter. Turn everything into a saucepan, preferably an enamel-lined one, and mix again. Bring to a boil, then reduce the heat to very low. Simmer without a cover, stirring frequently, for 2 to 3 hours, or until the mixture is thick. The longer it cooks, the better. Store in sterilized jars or in the refrigerator. Let the chutney ripen for a few days before using.

UNCOOKED MANGO CHUTNEY

Uncooked chutneys are side dishes for Indian curries. They must be made only a short while before serving and will keep only a day in the refrigerator.

About 2 cups

1 ripe mango (about 1 pound)
2 tablespoons fresh lemon juice, or more
1 tablespoon grated or finely minced gingerroot
1 small clove garlic, mashed
½ teaspoon salt
½ cup grated fresh coconut
  Tabasco

Peel the mango. Cut the flesh into ¼- to ½-inch cubes. Put mango into a bowl, and sprinkle and toss with the lemon juice. Add the gingerroot, garlic, salt, and coconut, and mix well. Stir in Tabasco to taste, starting with about 3 drops. Check the flavor and add additional Tabasco, a few drops at a time, tasting as you go along to avoid excessive hotness. You may also want to add a little more lemon juice. Cover and refrigerate 10 minutes to 1 hour.

ENGLISH LEMON COMPOTE FOR HOT OR COLD ROAST FOWL

About 3 cups

6 fleshy, thin-skinned lemons
6 small sprays fresh tarragon or 2 tablespoons dried tarragon, or less to taste
2 cups sugar
2 cups water
Tabasco (optional)

With a sharp knife, pare the zest—the yellow part of the rind,—from 2 of the lemons. There should be no trace of the white pith that lies under the skin. Cut zest into fine strips and pour boiling water over them. Drain and reserve. Cut zest and all pith from the lemons. Cut lemons into thin rounds and remove seeds. Place slices in a shallow heatproof serving dish and scatter with tarragon. (If fresh tarragon is used, dip for a moment into boiling water.) Boil the sugar and water together for 3 or 4 minutes, or until thick. Add reserved lemon zest strips, and Tabasco to taste. Pour over lemon slices and chill. Drain off excessive liquid before serving.

SWEET-SOUR ONION COMPOTE

This absolutely delicious recipe was originally made by the famous French chef M. Michel Guérard. Serve it with pâtés and meatloaves.

About 3 cups

- 7 tablespoons sweet butter
- 7 cups thinly sliced onions (about 6 medium)
- 1½ cups confectioners' sugar
- 1 tablespoon salt
  Freshly ground white pepper
- ½ cup currants
- ½ cup wine vinegar
- ¼ cup dry red wine
- 3 tablespoons black currant liqueur or grenadine

Heat the butter in a Dutch oven. Add the onions and sauté over low to medium heat until tender, about 20 minutes, stirring occasionally. Regulate heat as necessary. Stir in the sugar, salt and pepper to taste. Cook over low heat for about 10 minutes, stirring occasionally. Sir in the currants, vinegar, wine, and liqueur. Simmer over low heat until flavors are blended, about 1 hour. Refrigerate until serving time. Reheat or serve cold.

Desserts

Whatever people say about them (not good for diets, too fattening, too full of sugar, unsophisticated eating, etcetera), desserts are here to stay—possibly because after a meal almost everyone craves a little something extra that is fun to eat and has no obligation to be nutritious. Guests especially feel deprived if they get no dessert, even if they protest that they never eat them. In my experience, these Spartans, when confronted with a little bit of lusciousness, will plunge into dessert with the best. Unlike simmering stews, baking bread, or roasting chickens, which attract with their aroma, desserts must have eye appeal to be fetching. Mashed raspberries taste good, but they don't look good.

Desserts don't have to be complicated. But they must be worth the eating or else it is not worthwhile to waste one's allotment of calories upon them. In this age of liberated women—though it is still basically a man's world—it must not be forgotten that almost all men are natural dessert eaters. Not for nothing do experienced heart-breakers (the Countess Du Barry, mistress of Louis XV comes to mind) coax their followers to partake of a sweet and elegant little kickshaw, prepared by their own hands, or so they say.

Desserts are fun to make, I think, because they show that one cares to take a little extra trouble to please. Personally, I prefer to end my meal with fruit in some form or another. But thinking back on the hundreds and hundreds of people I have cooked for in my life, I think that at least for festive occasions, people prefer chocolate *"pour la bonne bouche."* Thus, when in doubt, I make a chocolate dessert.

Here again I can only repeat that the desserts that follow are favorites; as you can see, I don't care much for pies or tarts, and that's the reason why you won't find any in this book.

IN PRAISE OF FRUIT COMPOTES

The flavoring and seasonings of fruit compotes depend on individual tastes. The French use vanilla for their apples, pears, peaches, and apricots; the Italian favor lemon rind. Spices such as mace, ginger, cloves, cinnamon, coriander, and nutmeg are other excellent flavorings, and so are wine and liqueurs. Fruit compotes can consist of either one fruit or a combination. When combinations are used, it is better to cook each fruit separately. The drained fruits are combined in the serving dish, and their syrups boiled together until thickened by evaporation. Then they are poured over the fruits.

BASIC METHOD

For each pound or quart of fruit, use—generally speaking—1 cup sugar and 1 cup water, plus the flavoring of your choice. Make a syrup by boiling the sugar, water, and flavorings in a covered saucepan for 5 to 10 minutes. Add the washed fruit, a few pieces at a time, and poach over medium heat until done. Remove with a slotted spoon and repeat process until all fruit is used. If syrup is too thin, boil rapidly until the right consistency is achieved. Pour over fruit and serve hot or chilled, with or without cream.

Apples and blackberries (also good in pies)
Apricots, peaches, and plums
Apricots and strawberries
Blueberries and peaches
Cherries (these are best stewed by themselves)
Pears and bananas
Raspberries and pineapple
Strawberries and rhubarb

IMPROVED FRUIT COMPOTES

Fruit compotes are often vastly improved if a little liqueur is added to the syrup before it is poured over the fruit. Any domestic or imported liqueurs or cordials are admirably suited to the purpose. Suit your own taste, but at least at the beginning, go very, very easy on strongly flavored liqueurs (i.e. Pernod, anisette, Chartreuse), and be sure that others like their flavor as much as you do. Remember, some people do not like any alcohol in their foods, not even classic combinations like fresh pineapple and kirsch.

UNCOOKED BLUEBERRY COMPOTE WITH RED WINE

Serve with crisp cookies.

Serves 4 to 6

1 quart blueberries, picked over and washed
Sugar
Full-bodied dry red wine

Put the blueberries into a serving dish and add the sugar to taste. Add enough wine to barely cover the fruit. Chill thoroughly before serving.

CHESTNUTS WITH MARSALA AND WINE

An interesting dessert that can be eaten either hot or cold.

Serves 4 to 6

- 1 pound chestnuts
- ½ cup sugar
- 1 cup dry red wine
- 1 cup Marsala

Score the chestnuts across rounded side with a sharp knife. Place in boiling water and simmer for 15 minutes. Drain, but keep warm. Slip off both skins. The skins should come off quite easily, provided the chestnuts are warm. Work carefully, since chestnuts break very easily. Combine the sugar, red wine, and Marsala, and cook, covered, over low heat for 5 minutes. Carefully place chestnuts in wine mixture and simmer until tender. Shake pan occasionally so that chestnuts won't stick. Lift chestnuts with a slotted spoon and place in a glass or silver serving dish. Reduce syrup and pour over chestnuts. Serve with plain heavy cream and thin, crisp cookies.

FRESH FIGS FLAMBÉ

A simple but spectacular chafing dish dessert.

Serves 6

12 ripe figs (preferably purple figs)
1⅓ cups Cognac
1½ cups heavy cream, sweetened to taste

Carefully peel the figs and place them on a chafing dish. Prick each fig with a silver fork. Pour the Cognac over the figs. Light the lamp under the chafing dish. Let the figs heat through for 2 minutes or so. Flame the Cognac and shake the chafing dish gently until the flames die. Serve immediately, with a pitcher of heavy cream.

ORANGES À LA GRECQUE

*Very pretty to look at and perfectly delicious, with a fruit
that is always available.*

Serves 4 to 6

6 large navel oranges
3 cups sugar
4 cups water
  Few drops red food coloring or grenadine syrup

With a sharp knife, pare the zest—the orange part of the rind—from
the oranges. Cut zest into tiny strips with a pair of kitchen scissors.
Plunge strips into plenty of boiling water and boil for 2 minutes.
Drain. Repeat process twice, changing the water each time. (This is
to remove the bitterness from the zest.) Reserve zest. Peel off all the
pith—the white underskin—from the oranges so that none remains.
Use a very sharp knife, and hold oranges over the glass dish in
which they will be served to save juice. Cut 5 of the oranges in half
through their middle and remove seeds carefully. Separate the other
orange into sections and cover the bottom of the serving dish with
these sections. Put the orange halves on the sections, round side up.
Boil the sugar and water together for 10 minutes. Add enough food
coloring to give syrup a clear, red color. Pour the hot syrup over the
oranges and let stand 15 minutes. Drain off syrup and boil again for
15 minutes. Add zest to the oranges and pour hot syrup over all.
Cool, then chill in refrigerator 8 hours or overnight.

ITALIAN BAKED PEACHES

PESCHE RIPIENE

A classic Italian dessert. The peaches must be large and ripe but still firm. Freestone peaches are best.

Serves 4

4 large peaches
½ cup almond macaroon crumbs or ground almonds
¼ cup mixed glacé fruit, shredded fine
8 blanched almonds
 Marsala or white wine

Preheat the oven to moderate (350° F).

Halve the peaches. Remove pits and enlarge hollow slightly with a spoon. Mash this extra pulp and combine with the macaroon crumbs and glacé fruit. Fill peach hollows with this mixture. Butter a deep baking dish. Place peaches in 1 layer in the dish. Top each peach half with 1 almond. Sprinkle with Marsala or white wine. Bake for 15 to 20 minutes, or until just tender. Check for dryness; if necessary, add a little Marsala diluted with water, or some wine. Serve hot or cold.

SWISS PINEAPPLE AU KIRSCH

An average 2-pound pineapple will serve 4 persons and a very large one, 6 to 8. Fresh pineapple, one of the best desserts in the world, is still a luxury in Europe. Swiss hotels serve it constantly, doused with kirsch, the colorless and potent brandy made from cherry stones that is Switzerland's beloved and much-consumed drink. Kirsch is good on all fruit, and most invigorating when poured into black coffee, Swiss fashion.

Pineapple
Sugar
Kirsch

Cut off top and bottom of the pineapple. Cut into quarters (or eighths, if pineapple is large). Peel with a sharp knife, removing all eyes. Remove hard core. Cut into neat, even pieces. Add sugar and kirsch to taste. Chill thoroughly.

FRESH ITALIAN PLUM COMPOTE

Serves 4 to 6

½ cup sugar
1 cup dry red wine
1 lemon, with peel, cut into very thin slices, seeds removed
1½ pounds blue Italian plums, pitted

Combine the sugar, wine, and lemon slices in a saucepan. Stir to dissolve sugar. Bring to a boil. Add the plums to the syrup and cook for 3 minutes. Serve warm or chilled.

DELICIOUS RAISIN COMPOTE

A dish that has traveled from Lebanon to the Balkans, and deserves to come to American tables.

Serves 4

2 cups white raisins
1 cup water
1 cup honey
 Grated rind of 1 lemon
½ cup pine nuts

Soak the raisins in water to cover for 1 hour; drain. Boil together the water and honey for 2 to 3 minutes. Add the raisins and lemon rind, and simmer over low heat for 10 minutes. Skim with slotted spoon as needed. Add the pine nuts to raisins. Chill thoroughly before serving.

GLORIFIED WATERMELON

1 ripe watermelon
Brandy

Cut a deep plug from the watermelon and reserve the plug. Pour as much brandy into the watermelon as it will take. Replace the plug and seal with cellophane tape to keep the plug firmly in the melon. Chill for at least 8 hours.

Serve as usual, in wedges or slices. Avoid the part that was plugged for the sake of esthetics.

———

FRENCH CHOCOLATE AND RASPBERRY CREAM

You really don't need a recipe—just combine the ingredients to your taste in amounts needed.

Serves 6

2 cups heavy cream
½ teaspoon vanilla extract
¼ pound dark sweet eating chocolate, finely grated
¼ cup sugar (omit if frozen raspberries are used)
2 to 3 cups fresh raspberries or 2 10-ounce packages frozen raspberries, thawed and well drained

Whip the cream with the vanilla. Fold in the chocolate. Sprinkle the sugar on the fresh raspberries and fold into cream. Spoon into individual serving dishes or a glass dish. Chill thoroughly before serving, but do not refrigerate for more than 1 hour or cream will separate. The dessert is best made just before serving or just before the meal begins.

COCONUT CUSTARD

During the baking, the thick coconut milk rises to the top, leaving a custard below in the dish. This makes for a charming texture and flavor contrast. Once you have coconut milk, the dessert could not be easier. It can easily be doubled.

Serves 4

2 cups thick fresh coconut milk or cream, page 191
½ cup heavy cream
3 large eggs
¼ cup sugar
½ teaspoon almond extract
  Sweetened whipped cream

Preheat the oven to slow (325° F).

Combine the coconut milk and heavy cream in a heavy saucepan, and scald. Beat together the eggs, sugar, and almond extract in a 1- or 1½-quart baking dish. Gradually stir in the hot milk mixture. Set in a pan with 2 inches of hot water. Bake for 1 hour, or until a silver knife or a skewer inserted at the edge of the custard comes out clean. Cool before chilling. Serve with whipped cream on the side and any suitable fruit compote which is on the tart side, such as apricot, pineapple, or orange.

DUTCH LEMON CREAM

This cream can be prepared in advance, provided the egg whites are added just before serving time.

Serves 4

4 eggs, separated
½ cup sugar
   Grated rind of 1 large lemon
   Juice of 2 large lemons
½ cup dry white wine

Beat the egg yolks and sugar until thick in the top of a double boiler. Add the lemon rind. Stir in the lemon juice and wine. Cook mixture over hot (not boiling)water, beating constantly with a rotary beater until thick and stiff. Cool thoroughly. Beat egg whites until very stiff and fold gently into cream. Serve in sherbet glasses with small cookies.

SPANISH MILK PUDDING

DULCE DE LECHE

This must be of Moorish origin, since it is both very sweet and very spicy. A heavy saucepan is absolutely essential for the success of this dessert.

Serves 4

---

4 cups milk
2¼ cups sugar
2 tablespoons ground almonds
1 stick cinnamon

Combine all the ingredients in a heavy saucepan. Cook over medium heat, stirring constantly, until mixture thickens to consistency of a custard. Remove cinnamon. Pour into individual bowls. Chill thoroughly before serving with crisp cookies.

FRENCH CHOCOLATE MOUSSE

MOUSSE AU CHOCOLAT

The simplest and most elegant of all chocolate desserts.

Serves 5 to 8

½ pound dark sweet eating chocolate (not milk chocolate)
¼ cup cold water or coffee
5 eggs, separated
1 tablespoon rum, brandy, or kirsch

Combine the chocolate and cold water, and melt over hot water, or over very low heat, stirring constantly. Cool slightly. Add the egg yolks, one at a time, stirring until completely blended with chocolate. Stir in the rum. Beat egg whites until stiff but not dry. Fold carefully into chocolate mixture until just blended. Pile into small white soufflé dishes, pots de crème dishes, or sherbet glasses. (This amount will fill 5 to 8 cups, depending on size.) Chill overnight or at least 8 hours. The mousse must be thoroughly chilled and ripened to acquire the characteristic spongy consistency.

PINEAPPLE FLAN

Serves 4

1 8-ounce can crushed pineapple in its own juice
1¼ cups sugar
3 large eggs
3 tablespoons flour
1 tablespoon kirsch or light rum
1 teaspoon fresh lemon juice

Preheat the oven to moderate (350° F).

Set 4 6-ounce custard cups in oven. Remove 2 tablespoons of the pineapple from can and set aside. In a blender or food processor, whirl remaining pineapple and juice until pineapple is puréed. There should be about ¾ cup. In a small saucepan, combine puréed pineapple with ¾ cup of the sugar. Bring to a boil. Cook gently over low heat for 3 minutes. Add the reserved 2 tablespoons pineapple; cook for 2 more minutes. In a small bowl, beat the eggs lightly. Gradually beat in the flour, kirsch, and lemon juice. Beat until well blended and smooth. Stir in pineapple mixture and set aside. In a small saucepan, heat the remaining ½ cup sugar over low heat until sugar melts and turns a caramel color, swirling pan occasionally. Do not let burn. Using potholders and being careful, evenly divide caramel sauce among the hot custard cups. Quickly and carefully swirl caramel around in cups. Pour pineapple mixture over caramel sauce in cups, using a scant ½ cup mixture for each cup. Place cups in a 9-inch-square pan. Pour boiling water in pan around cups to a depth of ½ inch. Bake for 30 minutes, or until knife inserted in center comes out clean. Cool. To serve, loosen edges of custard. Invert onto serving dishes, allowing some of caramel sauce to cover custard.

THE EMPRESS'S RICE PUDDING

RIZ À L'IMPÉRATRICE

This rice dessert, named after the elegant and frivolous Empress Eugénie, wife of Napoleon III, can only be described as the rice pudding to end all rice puddings. It will end a special meal with éclat, the way a tableau ends a display of fireworks.

Serves 10

⅓ cup chopped citron
⅓ cup chopped candied lemon peel
⅓ cup chopped candied orange peel
½ cup kirsch
½ cup sugar
1 cup water
¾ cup rice
2 cups milk
1 2-inch piece vanilla bean or 1 tablespoon vanilla extract
2 envelopes (2 tablespoons) unflavored gelatin
2 cups heavy cream
   Red currant jelly
   Raspberry Sauce (see below)

Combine the citron, lemon peel, orange peel, and kirsch, and marinate for several hours or overnight.

Combine the sugar with ½ cup of the water and bring to a boil. Wash the rice and cook in the boiling sugar syrup for 5 minutes, stirring constantly. Drain rice and reserve syrup for use in other desserts. In the top of a double boiler, heat the milk and vanilla. Add rice and mix thoroughly. Cover and cook over boiling water for about 1 hour, or until almost all the milk is absorbed, stirring occasionally. The rice should be creamy but not liquid. Soften the gelatin in the remaining ½ cup water for 3 minutes, stirring occasionally. Add to hot rice. Blend thoroughly and cool the mixture. Whip the cream until stiff and blend with fruits and kirsch.

Add mixture to rice. Rinse a 2-quart mold with cold water. Line mold thinly with red currant jelly. Pack rice into mold and chill overnight. Unmold on a deep platter and serve with Raspberry Sauce and an egg custard sauce.

NOTE: One version of *riz à l'impératrice* adds 1 cup egg custard (any standard recipe) to the cooked rice before the gelatin is added. This makes for a creamier pudding. Personally, I prefer to serve the custard, which does belong to the *riz à l'impératrice*, separately, as sauce. In this case, I increase the amount of custard to 2 cups.

RASPBERRY SAUCE
2 10-ounce packages frozen raspberries
½ cup sugar
½ cup kirsch

Simmer together the raspberries with the sugar until raspberries are very soft. Strain through a sieve or whirl in an electric blender. Add the kirsch. Chill before serving.

STONE CREAM

Said to be one of Queen Victoria's favorites, and very famous among old English creams. The following very good recipe is taken verbatim from an old English cookbook that I found in an old inn at Muker, high up in northern England's wild and beautiful Pennine Mountains.

Serves 4 to 6

One pot of preserved apricots or plums [jam], half an ounce of isinglass [1 envelope (1 tablespoon) unflavored gelatin], one pint of cream [heavy cream], one lemon, two teaspoonfuls of crushed white sugar [1 tablespoon, or more or less].

Take a glass dish and line it at the bottom about an inch thick with preserved apricots or plums, dissolve half an ounce of isinglass in a little water [dissolve the gelatin, that is], add to it a pint of thick cream, the peel of the lemon grated, enough sugar to make pleasant to your taste. Let it boil one minute, then put it into a jug that has a spout. When it is nearly cold, but not quite set, squeeze into it the juice of the lemon [or rather, squeeze the lemon into a cup and then add it to the cream, lest a seed fall into the jug]. Pour it into the dish [from the jug with a spout] over the sweetmeat, and let it stand all night. Place on the top a few ratafias [small almond macaroons].

EN AVANT, intrepid cooks!

ZABAGLIONE

This is one of the world's great desserts. The combination of eggs, sugar, and spirits occurs in other countries besides Italy, but nowhere else is the formula so happy. In a pinch, sherry can be used instead of Marsala, but an authentic zabaglione must have Marsala.

Serves 3

4 egg yolks
¾ cup sugar
¾ cup Marsala, sweet or dry

Combine all the ingredients in the top of a double boiler. Cook over simmering (not boiling) water, beating constantly with a wire whisk or rotary beater, for about 10 minutes, or until very thick. Serve immediately in glasses or small coffee cups.

Baked Alaska

Called glace siberienne (*Siberian ice cream*) *in French, this fancy concoction will not fail to amaze when you want to impress the folks. It is not hard to make, but you have to work fast!*

Serves 12

1 to 2 tablespoons apricot preserves or honey
  About 12 vanilla-flavored cookies or enough thin slices of pound cake to cover a 7x5-inch area
2 to 3 tablespoons brandy
6 large egg whites (about ¾ cup)
¼ cup sugar
¼ teaspoon vanilla extract
½ gallon vanilla ice cream in 1 block, about 7x5 inches
¼ cup brandy
3 10-ounce packages quick-thaw mixed frozen fruit, thawed (about 3 cups) (optional)

Lightly spread enough preserves or honey to cover the bottom of the cookies or 1 side of pound cake slices. Place the cookies, preserve or honey side down, side by side in the center of a bread board or baking sheet lined with heavy brown paper to form a rectangle about 7x5 inches. This will form a base for the ice cream. Sprinkle cookies or cake with 2 to 3 tablespoons brandy and place in freezer.

In the large bowl of an electric mixer, beat the egg whites until foamy, using low speed. Gradually add the sugar, increasing speed to high. Beat until stiff peaks form. Fold in the vanilla. Quickly remove the ice cream from container. Place ice cream on cookie or cake rectangle, centering ice cream so cookies are completely covered. Quickly spread egg white mixture evenly over ice cream and cookie edges right down to paper; freeze solid. Before serving, bake in center of preheated hot (500° F) oven about 2 minutes or until meringue is lightly browned. Meanwhile, in a small saucepan, heat ¼ cup brandy until warm. When meringue is lightly browned, remove from oven. Quickly pour heated brandy over meringue; ignite brandy. When flames subside, cut in slices using knife dipped in warm water. Serve with the mixed fruit if desired.

NOTE: The brandy must be heated; it won't flame if cold. Flaming is best done at the table. You can heat the brandy in the kitchen and bring it out with the Baked Alaska.

BISCUIT TORTONI

Biscuit Tortoni used to be a standard dessert in Italian restaurants before Italian restaurants became as high-flown as so many are today. The dessert is easy to make, pleasant to eat, and unassuming after a rich meal.

Serves 6 to 8

2 eggs, separated
½ cup sifted confectioners' sugar
3 tablespoons rum or brandy
½ cup crushed almond macaroons
¼ cup finely chopped glacé fruit
1 cup heavy cream, whipped
3 tablespoons coarsely ground blanched almonds

Beat the egg yolks until fluffy. Beat in the sugar a little at a time, beating well after each addition. Stir in the rum. Stir in the almond macaroons and glacé fruit. Fold the whipped cream into the mixture. Beat the egg whites until stiff but not dry and fold into the mixture. Spoon equal amounts of the mixture into 4-ounce paper cupcake cups or into individual serving dishes. Sprinkle each with the almonds. Cover with plastic wrap (or dessert will absorb freezer flavors) and freeze until firm. Serve in the paper cups if used.

FROZEN ROMAN PUNCH

An Italian-style sorbet.

Serves 4 to 6 (About 1 quart)

1 cup water
1 cup sugar
¼ cup sparkling wine or dry white wine
⅓ cup fresh lemon juice
¼ cup orange juice
1 egg white
¼ cup confectioners' sugar
¼ cup rum

Pour the water into a saucepan and stir in the sugar. Boil for 5 minutes over low heat until the sugar is totally dissolved. Remove from heat and cool for 5 minutes. Add the sparkling wine, lemon juice, and orange juice. Cover the saucepan and let stand at room temperature for 1 hour. Prepare the ice cream freezer as usual with ice and coarse salt. Spoon the sugar mixture into the container, close it tightly, and freeze until solid. Or turn into a 1-quart ice cube tray and freeze in refrigerator freezer until firm. Beat the egg white with the confectioners' sugar until the mixture is stiff and glossy. Break up frozen mixture and quickly beat until smooth. Fold in beaten egg white mixture. Slowly stir in the rum. Return to freezer and continue freezing until solid. Serve in sherbet glasses, preferably with a little sprig of fresh mint.

ORANGE PEEL CANDY

An old recipe from my grandmother.

Orange peel from 8 oranges, yellow part only, very thinly cut
⅓ cup (approximately) slivered blanched almonds
⅞ cup (approximately) honey
¼ cup sugar

Weigh the peel first; use the same amount of honey and about one-fifth of the peel's weight in almonds. Cut the orange peel into julienne strips. Put it into a bowl and add enough cold water to cover. Let the peel soak for two days, changing the water at least once daily; this will remove the bitter taste of the peel and soften it. Toast the slivered almonds lightly in a preheated moderate (350° F) oven for 5 minutes.

Drain the peel and squeeze it dry in a kitchen towel. Pour the honey into a saucepan and add the orange peel. Cook over low heat, stirring constantly with a wooden spoon, for about 20 to 30 minutes, to coat the orange peel thoroughly with the honey. Add the almonds and cook for 5 minutes longer, stirring all the time. Then stir in the sugar and remove from the heat. Pour the mixture onto a large flat serving dish or cookie sheet. Cut the candy into desired shapes. Serve as is. Or else the candy may be sprinkled with silver shot while still warm, cut into shapes, and wrapped in paper. It should be eaten within a few days.

AUTHENTIC ATHOLE BROSE

From a Dewar's Scotch whisky ad.

Serves 4 to 6

Athole is a small town in the craggy mountains near Perth, Scotland; brose is the Scottish word for brew. Athole Brose is a Scotch drink concocted many years ago to warm the festive soul on important occasions such as St. Andrew's Day (Scotland's patron saint), Christmas, and Hogmanay (New Year's Eve). You may use any good strong Scotch whisky for the dish.

    1 cup honey (preferably heather honey from Scotland)
    1½ to 2 cups heavy cream
    2 cups Dewar's White Label Scotch whisky

Heat the honey, and when it thins slightly, stir in the cream. Heat together, but do not let boil. Remove from heat and slowly stir in the Scotch whisky. Athole Brose may be served hot or chilled.

NOTE: If you would like even a little more touch of Scotland, soak 1 cup oatmeal in two cups water overnight. Strain and mix liquid with other ingredients.

QUICK BABA AU RHUM

True babas are made with a yeast dough. This very easy and acceptable version was given to me many years ago by the cook of a French friend who lived on the Île St.-Louis in Paris.

Serves 8

1 cup all-purpose flour, lightly spooned into cup
1 teaspoon baking powder
¼ teaspoon salt
2 large eggs, separated
½ cup sugar
⅓ cup butter, melted and cooled
1 teaspoon vanilla extract
  Rum Syrup (see below)

Preheat the oven to moderate (375° F).

In a small bowl, mix together the flour, baking powder, and salt; reserve. In the small bowl of an electric mixer, beat the egg whites until foamy. Gradually add ¼ cup of the sugar, increasing speed to high and beating until stiff peaks form; reserve. Using same beaters in another bowl, beat the egg yolks thoroughly with the remaining ¼ cup sugar until sugar is thoroughly blended. Fold yolk mixture into egg whites just until blended. Gently and lightly fold flour mixture into egg mixture until flour mixture is blended. Gently and lightly fold in the butter and vanilla. Using about ¼ cup batter for each baba, spoon batter into 8 buttered 2¾x2x1⅛-inch muffin cups. Bake for about 15 minutes, or until a skewer inserted in center of babas comes out clean. Loosen sides of babas. With fork, carefully prick each baba several times. Spoon about a scant ¼ cup Rum Syrup over each baba. When all syrup has been absorbed by babas, carefully lift babas out of pan using a knife or spatula.

RUM SYRUP

1 cup sugar
1 cup water
½ cup light or dark rum

In a small saucepan combine the sugar and water. Bring to a boil and boil for 5 minutes. Remove from heat and stir in the rum.

BEIGNETS SOUFFLÉS

The less elegant French name for these delicious fried puffs is pets-de-nonnes. *More delicate French souls call them* soupirs-de-nonnes.

Serves 4 or 5 (About 20 pieces)

Oil for deep-frying (preferably peanut)
½ cup water
¼ cup butter
⅛ teaspoon salt
½ cup flour
2 large eggs
½ cup confectioners' sugar

Pour oil into a large saucepan or deep-fryer to a depth of about 3 inches. Heat to 375° F. In a small saucepan, bring the water and butter to a boil. Add the salt. Remove from heat and add the flour all at once. Beat vigorously until mixture forms a ball. Add 1 egg. Beat vigorously and well until mixture is smooth. Add the remaining egg. Beat well until smooth. If desired, this procedure may be done in a food processor. Drop batter by tablespoonfuls, a few at a time, into the oil. Deep-fry for about 7 minutes, or until golden brown and done in the center. Batter will sink to the bottom, then will rise to the surface of the oil. Remove with a slotted spoon and drain on paper towels; keep warm. When all are fried, transfer to a serving plate lined with a doily. Serve warm sprinkled with the confectioners' sugar.

CARRÉ DE CONFITURE

From Betty Boulpaep, an inspired Belgian cook. Like all puff pastry desserts, the pastry should be fresh and crisp.

Serves 8 or 9

1 10-ounce package frozen patty shells, thawed
1 12-ounce jar apricot preserves, heated slightly
1 egg, beaten

Preheat the oven to moderate (375 F).

Stack 3 patty shells on a work surface and pinch edges together. Roll out to a 10-inch square. Place in center of a large ungreased baking sheet, preferably a sheet with a lip or short sides. Using a fork, prick pastry many times. Evenly spread on three quarters of the apricot preserves (about ¾ cup) to within ¼ inch of edge. Roll out remaining 3 patty shells as above and cut square diagonally into ½-inch-wide strips. Arrange strips side by side over apricot-covered pastry. Trim edges. Firmly press the edges of strips down to bottom square to firmly seal. Brush strips with some of the egg. Bake for about 30 minutes, or until golden brown. After about 15 minutes of baking, prick pastry several times with a fork. Brush on remaining preserves (about ¼ cup). With wide spatula loosen edges of pastry, then the center. Slide pastry onto a rack or work surface to cool. Cut into 9 squares.

EUROPEAN FRUIT FRITTERS

Fruit fritters are a favorite dessert the length and breadth of Europe. They are easy to make, especially with an electric deep-fryer that controls the temperature. The procedure is always the same: the fruit is pitted, sprinkled with sugar and any desired spices such as cinnamon, cloves, ginger, etc., and allowed to stand for about 30 minutes. Then it is drained and dried between paper towels. The drying is a very important step, for if the fruit is not well dried, the batter will not cling to it and the fruit will ooze out when frying. Next the fruit is dipped into the batter and the excess shaken off. It is then fried, a few pieces at a time, in deep oil or other fat heated to 375° F for 2 to 3 minutes, or until golden brown. The fritters are drained on paper towels, sprinkled with sugar, and served immediately. Canned fruit is treated in the same manner. To my taste, the best fritters are made with plums, cherries, apricots, oranges, apples, peaches, bananas, and pineapple, in that order.

FRENCH FRITTER BATTER FOR FRUITS

This is a very light and airy batter, thanks to the beer and the extra egg white. There is no taste of beer whatsoever in the finished fritter.

About 1 cup

½ cup flour
¼ teaspoon salt
1 tablespoon melted butter
1 egg, well beaten
½ cup beer
1 egg white, stiffly beaten

Sift together the flour and salt. Blend the batter and egg and add to flour. Stir in the beer gradually, stirring only until mixture is smooth. Let stand in warm place for 1 to 2 hours, until batter is light and foamy. When ready to use, fold in beaten egg white.

"MISERABLE"

This is recreated from a tasty, rich specialty of Brussels's famous Pâtisserie Whittamer, where every morsel is heavenly.

Serves 10 to 12

1¼ cups ground blanched almonds (about 1 cup whole almonds, ground)
1¼ cups sugar
 1 tablespoon cornstarch
 6 large egg whites (about ¾ cup)
   Dash salt
 ¼ cup water
 3 large egg yolks
 1 cup sweet butter, at room temperature
 3 tablespoons brandy
 ¼ cup confectioners' sugar

MERINGUE

Preheat the oven to slow (250° F).

In a small bowl, combine well the almonds, ¾ cup of the sugar, and the cornstarch; set aside. Grease 1 large baking sheet (at least 12 inches wide) or 2 regular-size baking sheets; dust with flour and shake off excess. In the large bowl of an electric mixer, combine the egg whites and salt. Beat at low speed until foamy. Gradually increase speed to high and beat until egg whites form stiff peaks. Fold in almond-sugar mixture. Using half of the mixture, drop dollops of egg white mixture onto 1 side of large baking sheet or 1 regular-size baking sheet to form outer edges of a 10x5-inch rectangle. Fill center of rectangle with egg white mixture. With a spatula, smooth surface to obtain a 10x5-inch rectangle of even thickness. Repeat procedure with remaining egg white mixture; you should have 2 10x5-inch rectangles side by side on 1 large baking sheet or 1 10x5-inch rectangle on each of 2 regular-size baking sheets. Bake for 55 to 60 minutes, or until meringue is lightly browned. With a wide spatula, carefully loosen rectangles from baking sheet or sheets, washing off spatula occasionally with cold water as each side of rectangles and centers are loosened. (Shake excess water off spatula.) Carefully slide each rectangle onto wax paper. Cool thoroughly.

FILLING

In a small saucepan, bring the remaining ½ cup sugar and the water to a boil. Boil for 2 minutes; then cool. In the small bowl of an electric mixer, lightly beat the egg yolks. Gradually add sugar syrup, beating at high speed. When all of sugar syrup has been added, beat at high speed for 5 minutes, scraping bowl occasionally. Yolk mixture will become thick and double in volume, and will be pale yellow in color. Gradually beat in small amounts of the butter, alternating butter with the brandy. After all butter and brandy have been added, beat until smooth, about 1 to 2 minutes, scraping sides of bowl occasionally.

To assemble, place 1 meringue rectangle on a serving plate bottom side down. Spoon on filling. With a spatula, spread filling evenly about ½ inch thick. Top with remaining meringue rectangle, bottom side up. The dessert should be under 2 inches thick. Chill for 2 hours. To serve, trim edges with a serrated knife. Dust top with the confectioners' sugar.

DESSERT ORANGE CAKE

This different and easy to make cake is wonderful. The recipe is one of Sephardic cookery, one of the most interesting cuisines of the Mediterranean.

Serves 8 to 10

2 large thin-skinned juice oranges
1 cup sugar
½ pound blanched almonds (about 1½ cups)
6 large eggs, separated
1 tablespoon rose water (optional)
Confectioners' sugar or whipped cream

Preheat the oven to moderate (350° F).

Butter and flour a 10-inch springform pan with removable bottom. Scrub the oranges, and scrub off any price stamps or markings. Place the oranges in a large saucepan with a tight-fitting lid and add enough water to come halfway up the oranges. Cook, covered, over medium heat for about 1 hour, or until the oranges are very soft and can easily be pierced with a fork. Remove oranges from water and let them cool thoroughly. When cool, cut into quarters and remove the seeds. With a sharp knife—or, much better, in a food processor—chop the peel and pulp of the oranges very fine. Transfer to a large bowl and reserve. In a blender or food processor, grind together ½ cup of the sugar and the blanched almonds until the consistency of coarse flour. Add the mixture to the oranges in the bowl and stir in the remaining ½ cup sugar, mixing well. Beat the egg yolks into the batter one at a time, mixing well after each addition. Stir in the rose water. Beat the egg whites until stiff but not dry and fold them gently into the batter. Spoon into prepared springform pan. Bake for 1 hour, or until the top of the cake is slightly browned and the cake feels firm but not hard. Cool the cake on a rack. Run a knife along the side of the cake, and release and remove the ring. Cool the cake completely before trying to remove the bottom of the pan. (Since the cake is fragile and moist, it is better to serve it from the pan bottom.) Before serving, sift a little confectioners' sugar over the top of the cake or decorate the top with rosettes of whipped cream.

PARADISE CAKE

TORTA PARADISO

A standby of Italian cakes.

Serves 6 to 8

1½ cups butter
1½ cups sugar
    Grated rind of 1 lemon
  8 egg yolks
1¼ cups flour
 ⅞ cup potato starch
  3 egg whites
    Confectioners' sugar

Preheat the oven to moderate (350° F).

Cream the butter with a wooden spoon or electric mixer until very soft. Beat in the sugar. Stir in the lemon rind and egg yolks, one by one. Sift together the flour and potato starch, and sprinkle onto the butter mixture gradually, folding the mixture into the batter as you sprinkle it on. Beat the egg whites until stiff and fold them gently into the batter. Butter and flour an 8-inch springform pan. Spoon in the batter; it should only fill the pan halfway. Bake for about 45 to 55 minutes, or until the center of the cake tests done. Remove the cake from the pan and cool it either on a cake rack or on a clean kitchen towel. Sift confectioners' sugar over the top. This exquisite cake will keep fresh for several days if wrapped in plastic wrap or aluminum foil. (The batter may also be dropped by spoonfuls onto a greased baking sheet, allowing room for spreading. Bake in a preheated moderate [350° F] oven for about 10 minutes.) Serve with cappuccino (espresso coffee and hot milk) or a cup of hot chocolate.

NOTE: This cake, which has a very fine, close-grain texture, is a specialty of a well-known pastry shop in Pavia. The shop jealously guards the recipe, which is almost a hundred years old. The recipe above is one of many imitations of the original current in today's home cooking.

PITHIVIERS

*A very French cake or pie of an almond filling encased in
puff paste, which must be fresh and crisp. I adore it, in spite
of the bother it is to make. Pithiviers is named after the
French town of the same name.*

Serves 8 to 10

4 large egg yolks
2 large eggs
½ cup sugar
1 cup ground blanched almonds (about ¾ cup whole almonds,
   ground)
¼ cup rum
1 10-ounce package frozen patty shells, thawed
1 egg, beaten
1 tablespoon sugar (preferably superfine)

Preheat the oven to hot (450° F).

In the large bowl of an electric mixer, mix together with a fork the
egg yolks, whole eggs, and sugar. Beat together at high speed for 5
minutes until mixture has thickened, increased in volume, and is
pale yellow in color. Fold in the almonds and rum; set aside. Stack 3
patty shells on a work surface and pinch edges together. Roll out to
about a 12-inch circle. Press into a 9-inch pie plate; pastry should
completely cover bottom, sides, and lip of pie plate. Pour in almond
filling. Roll out remaining 3 patty shells as above, rolling pastry to
an 11-inch circle. Carefully center and lay pastry over filling. With
fingers, firmly pinch edge of top pastry to edge of bottom pastry to
firmly seal. Flute the edges. Using some of the beaten egg, lightly
brush the pastry, including the edges. Using a toothpick, prick
pastry several times. Bake for about 15 minutes, or until golden
brown. Cake will puff. If necessary, prick pastry a few more times
during baking. Remove from oven. Sprinkle the cake with 1 tablespoon sugar. Reduce the heat to 350° F and bake for 5 more minutes.
Cool. To serve, cut in wedges using a serrated knife.

CENTRAL EUROPEAN PLUM TART

Middle Europeans are extremely fond of open fruit tarts, which take the place of our fruit pies, but which I feel are more festive. All sorts of fruits are used, such as apples, pears, gooseberries, peaches, apricots, cherries, and plums, the latter two being the favorites. The recipe that follows can be adapted to all of these fruits, though of course the sugar has to be adjusted, depending on the tartness of the fruit.

Serves 6

1 cup flour
2 teaspoons baking powder
½ teaspoon salt
1 tablespoon sugar
3 tablespoons butter
⅓ cup milk
½ cup ground filberts or fine dry bread crumbs (optional, see Note)
1 to 1½ pounds plums, pitted and halved
2 egg yolks
⅔ cup heavy cream
⅓ cup sugar
½ cup chopped blanched almonds
¼ teaspoon ground nutmeg

Preheat the oven to hot (450° F).

Butter and flour a shallow 8- or 9-inch cake pan, preferably one with a removable bottom. Sift together the flour, baking powder, salt, and sugar. With a pastry blender or two knives, cut in the butter until the mixture resembles coarse meal. Add the milk and mix just long enough to combine the ingredients. Spread dough in bottom and on sides of pan. Crimp sides with the tines of a fork. Sprinkle with ground filberts if used. Arrange the plum halves, skin side down, over dough in concentric circles; the plum halves should overlap slightly. Beat together the egg yolks, heavy cream, sugar, almonds, and nutmeg. Spoon mixture over plums. Bake for 10 to 15 minutes, or until done. The topping should be set and golden brown.

NOTE: The ground filberts or fine dry bread crumbs will absorb any excess moisture from the fruit and keep the pastry dry.

SYDELL SCHWARTZ'S PASSOVER WALNUT CAKE

One of the world's great cakes, but it must be made with Passover cake meal (available where kosher foods are sold) for its wonderful smoothness. Be sure to grease and not to butter the cake pan if you serve the cake on Passover.

Serves 12

9 eggs, separated
1 cup sugar
2 tablespoons cake meal
1 teaspoon vanilla extract
⅛ teaspoon salt
2 cups shelled walnuts, ground
  Confectioners' sugar (optional)

Preheat the oven to moderate (350° F).

Grease and flour a 10-inch angel food pan with a removable bottom. Beat the egg yolks until foamy. Beat in the sugar, 2 tablespoons at a time, beating well after each addition. Beat in the cake meal, and stir in the vanilla and salt. Blend thoroughly. Stir in the walnuts. Beat the egg whites until stiff but not dry and fold them gently into the batter. Turn batter into pan and smooth out top. Bake for about 45 to 50 minutes, or until the cake tests done and shrinks away from the sides of the pan. Turn pan upside down and place over the neck of a bottle to cool. When cool, run a knife around the edges of the cake and around the tube, and turn the cake onto a cake platter. If desired, sift a little confectioners' sugar over the cake.

TRIFLE OR TIPSY CAKE

Serves 4 to 6

1 9-inch sponge cake, homemade or bought
⅔ cup raspberry or apricot jam
1½ cups medium dry sherry
4 egg yolks, beaten
2 tablespoons sugar
2 cups milk, scalded
½ teaspoon almond extract
½ cup heavy cream, whipped
  About ½ toasted slivered blanched almonds (available commercially) or 12 whole almonds, split and toasted
  Glacé cherries (optional)

Cut the sponge cake in half horizontally and place half in the dish from which the trifle will be served. Spread with the jam and top with the other cake half. Pour the sherry over the sponge cake. Let stand for 1 hour. If the cake looks dry, sprinkle more sherry on it; it should be moist.

Make a custard by combining the egg yolks and sugar in the top of a double boiler. Beat well. Place over (not in) hot water. Stir the scalded milk gradually into the egg mixture. Cook, stirring constantly with a wooden spoon, until the mixture thickens and coats the spoon. Do not overcook or the custard will curdle. Remove from heat and stir in the almond extract. Pour the hot custard over the sponge cake. Chill thoroughly.

At serving time, either pipe the whipped cream on the cake or simply cover the cake with it. Decorate with almonds and with the glacé cherries, cut in half, if using.

NOTE: A simpler trifle can be made by substituting the egg custard with commercial vanilla pudding, prepared with 2½ cups milk.

INEZ KUBLY'S SUPER DEVIL'S FOOD

This fine, very chocolaty cake was served to me many years ago by the wife of a Wisconsin cheese maker. The lady made hers with cheese rennet, but it works equally well with sour cream.

Serves 12

¾ cup Dutch-processed cocoa (no substitute)
1¾ cups sugar
4 eggs
½ cup milk
½ cup unsalted butter
2 cups sifted flour
1 teaspoon baking powder
1 teaspoon baking soda
½ teaspoon salt
1 cup sour cream (no substitute)
1 teaspoon vanilla extract
¼ teaspoon almond extract

Preheat the oven to moderate (350° F).

Butter and flour 3 8-inch layer cake pans. In the top of a double boiler, combine the cocoa, ¾ cup of the sugar, 1 egg yolk, and the milk. Cook over (not in) gently boiling water, stirring constantly until the mixture is thick. (Or use a small heavy saucepan and very low heat, taking care not to burn the ingredients.) Cool the mixture. Cream the butter until soft and fluffy. Gradually beat in the remaining cup of sugar, beating well after each addition. Beat in 1 whole egg and 2 egg yolks. Blend thoroughly. Sift the flour with the baking powder, baking soda, and salt. Beginning and ending with flour, add the flour and sour cream alternately to the butter mixture. Beat in the cocoa mixture, and the vanilla and almond extracts. Beat the remaining 3 egg whites until stiff but not dry. Fold gently into the batter. Spoon equal amounts of the batter into the prepared cake pans. Bake for about 30 minutes, or until the cake tests done and shrinks away from the sides of the pans. Do not overbake, since cake should be moist. Cool completely and frost as desired or spread layers with apricot jam, or raspberry or currant jelly, and top and sides with sweetened whipped cream.

3-MINUTE FUDGE CAKE

This excellent, quick, and easy recipe appeared many years ago on the Arm and Hammer baking soda package; people still write in for it. Yes, I know the cake takes more than 3 minutes to make, but still. . . .

Serves 6

  2 eggs
1½ cups firmly packed dark brown sugar
  2 squares (2 ounces) unsweetened baking chocolate, melted
  2 cups sifted cake flour
  1 teaspoon baking soda
 ½ teaspoon salt
 ¼ cup white vinegar
 ¾ cup milk
  1 teaspoon vanilla extract
 ½ cup butter or margarine, softened

Preheat the oven to moderate (350° F).

Butter and flour 2 8-inch layer cake pans or a 13x9x2-inch pan. Have all the ingredients at room temperature. In a large deep bowl, using an electric beater at high speed, beat together the eggs, brown sugar, and chocolate for 1 minute. (Or beat energetically by hand for 3 minutes.) Sift together the flour, baking soda, and salt. Combine the vinegar, milk, and vanilla. Add the flour, half the milk mixture, and the butter to the egg, sugar, and chocolate mixture. Beat for 1 minute with an electric beater or 3 minutes by hand. Add the remaining milk mixture and beat again for 1 minute. Spoon equal amounts of the batter into the prepared cake pans. Bake for about 45 minutes, or until the cake tests done and shrinks away from the sides of the pans. Cool completely and frost as desired.

CHOCOLATE GÂTEAU

A flat, rich cake from Nancy, in France.

Serves 6 to 8

4 squares (4 ounces) unsweetened baking chocolate
¼ cup water or coffee
½ cup sugar
½ cup butter, at room temperature and cut into pieces
3 large or 4 small eggs, separated
¼ cup ground or finely chopped nuts
2 tablespoons kirsch or 1 teaspoon vanilla extract
⅓ cup sifted flour
   Apricot jam or currant jelly
1 cup heavy cream, whipped

Preheat the oven to moderate (350° F).

Butter and flour 2 8-inch layer cake pans. Combine the chocolate and water in the top of a double boiler. Melt over (not in) hot water, stirring occasionally to make a smooth paste. Stir in the sugar and stir until it is melted. Remove the double boiler top from heat. Stir in the butter. Cool the mixture, stirring occasionally. Beat in the egg yolks, one at a time, beating well after each addition. Stir in the nuts and kirsch. Stir in the flour and mix well. Beat the egg whites until stiff and fold into the mixture. Spoon equal amounts of the batter into the prepared cake pans. Bake for about 20 to 30 minutes, or until the cake tests done. Do not overbake. Cool on cake racks. Put the 2 layers together sandwich-fashion with apricot jam. Frost top and sides with the whipped cream.

GIANDUIA CHOCOLATE CAKE

TORTA GIANDUIA

This excellent, impressive cake is one of the most famous of all Italian cakes. The word "Gianduia" identifies its Piedmontese origin. This cake is the pride of all the best pasticcerie—pastry shops—in a city and is seldom made at home. Maraschino is a very popular sweet cherry liqueur.

Serves 10 to 12

1¾ cups sugar
 ½ cup hazelnuts
 9 eggs
 1 tablespoon honey
 1 teaspoon vanilla extract
12 squares (¾ pound) semisweet baking chocolate
 ½ cup butter
 1 cup sifted cake flour
 1 cup sifted potato starch or cornstarch
10 tablespoons heavy cream
 2 tablespoons apricot jam
 ½ cup maraschino liqueur
 ¼ cup brandy
 8 squares (½ pound) sweet baking chocolate, melted in ¼ cup water

Preheat the oven to moderate (350° F).

Generously butter and flour a 10-inch springform pan. Melt 2 tablespoons of the sugar in a small heavy skillet over low heat, then add the hazelnuts. Coat hazelnuts on all sides with the sugar. Turn them out on wax paper and cool. Grind the hazelnuts in a blender or nutmill, or pound to a powder with a mortar and pestle.

Put into the top of a double boiler 6 whole eggs, 3 egg yolks, and 1¼ cups of the sugar. Beat together with a wire whisk. Over hot (not boiling) water, continue to beat the mixture until it is very thick and has begun to rise. Be careful that the mixture remains just lukewarm; if it heats up further, the cake will be ruined. Remove from heat and beat in the honey and vanilla. Continue beating until the mixture is cold and very thick and puffy. Grate 3 squares of the semisweet chocolate. Add with the butter and the ground hazelnuts to the top of a double boiler. Cook over hot (not boiling) water until the chocolate has melted, stirring until the mixture is perfectly smooth. Remove from heat and cool. Meanwhile, sift together the cake flour and the potato starch. Fold into the egg mixture. Stir in the chocolate mixture. Beat the remaining 3 egg whites until very stiff. Fold them into the batter. Turn batter into prepared pan. Bake for about 45 minutes, or until the cake tests done. Cool cake thoroughly on a rack.

Melt the remaining 9 squares semisweet chocolate in the top of a double boiler. Stir in ½ cup of the cream. Cook over hot (not boiling) water, stirring constantly until the mixture begins to boil. Remove from heat and cool. Stir frequently to prevent a skin from forming on the top. Stir in the apricot jam. Beat the mixture as if whipping cream. Put cake on a sheet of wax paper. Trim off all the loose crumbs. Cut cake in half horizontally. Combine the maraschino liqueur and brandy, and sprinkle half the mixture on each half of the cake. Reserve 4 tablespoons of the chocolate-cream-apricot jam mixture. Smoothly spread remaining jam mixture on 1 cake half. Top with the other cake half. Spread the top of the cake thinly with reserved jam mixture. To glaze cake, with a metal spatula spread the sides and top of the cake with the melted sweet baking chocolate to make a very smooth surface. Transfer the cake to a cake plate. Whip the remaining 2 tablespoons cream and put into a pastry bag. With a firm hand, write "Gianduia" on the cake. Or use prepared chocolate frosting. Refrigerate cake until serving time.

CHOCOLATE SOUR CREAM FROSTING

This simple and delicious frosting was invented by the late Helen Brown, an outstanding West Coast cook and cookbook writer; her books are worth searching for.

About ¾ cup

5 squares (5 ounces) semisweet baking chocolate
⅛ teaspoon salt
½ cup sour cream

In the top of a double boiler, melt the chocolate over (not in) gently boiling water, stirring until smooth. Stir in the salt. Remove the double boiler top from heat and stir until completely cooled. Beat in the sour cream and beat until the mixture is very smooth. Use immediately.

SIMPLE CHOCOLATE FROSTING

About ½ cup

2 squares (2 ounces) semisweet baking chocolate
2 tablespoons water, coffee, rum, or brandy
6 tablespoons butter, at room temperature and cut into pieces

In the top of a double boiler, melt the chocolate over (not in) gently boiling water, stirring until smooth. Remove the double boiler top from heat. Stir in the butter, a piece at a time, beating after each addition until the butter has been completely incorporated. Beat mixture until it has cooled and is of spreading consistency. Use immediately.

ALMOND COOKIES

These cookies are bland, appealing to people who don't like very sweet things. They are good with fruit and fruit compotes.

About 5 dozen 1½-inch cookies

- ¼ cup sifted confectioners' sugar
- ½ cup butter
- 1 egg yolk
- 1 teaspoon vanilla extract
- 2¼ cups sifted flour
- ¾ cup ground blanched almonds (about ½ cup whole almonds, ground)
- 1 beaten egg yolk

Preheat oven to moderate (350° F).

Beat together the sugar and butter until very soft. Stir in the egg yolk and vanilla, and mix thoroughly. Sift in the flour and mix. Add the almonds and knead to a smooth paste. Wrap in wax paper and chill for 3 hours. Between sheets of wax paper, roll out the dough to a thickness of ¼ inch. Cut with small cookie cutters or with a small glass dipped in flour. Transfer to an ungreased baking sheet. Brush with the egg yolk. Bake for about 10 to 12 minutes, or until barely golden. Cool on the baking sheet until cool enough to handle. Cool completely before storing in airtight containers.

HARTE BISSEN

My mother called these butterless hard cookies "hard morsels." They keep well in an airtight container.

About 25 cookies

1½ cups sifted flour
 1 teaspoon ground cinnamon
 ½ teaspoon ground cloves
 2 eggs
 ⅔ cup sugar
 ¼ cup finely ground filberts or walnuts
 ⅓ cup slivered blanched almonds
 ¼ cup finely chopped mixed glacé fruit
 1 tablespoon fresh lemon juice
    Thin Lemon Frosting (see below)

Sift together the flour, cinnamon, and cloves. Beat the eggs and sugar together until thick. Gradually beat the flour mixture into the egg mixture. Add the filberts, almonds, glacé fruit, and lemon juice. With your hands, knead the mixture until smooth. The dough should be firm; if too crumbly, knead in a little more flour 1 tablespoon at a time. Let the dough stand uncovered at room temperature overnight.

At baking time, preheat the oven to moderate (350° F).

On a floured surface, roll out the dough to a thickness of ¼ inch. Cut the dough into strips about 3 inches long and ½ inch wide, and place the strips on greased and floured baking sheets. Bake for about 25 minutes, or until golden brown. While still warm, frost with Thin Lemon Frosting.

THIN LEMON FROSTING

To each 1 cup sifted confectioners' sugar, add 1 or 2 tablespoons lemon juice. Stir until smooth. If desired, add 1 or 2 drops of food coloring to tint the frosting.

PFEFFERNUESSE

Let these ripen in a covered container for 1 to 2 weeks for a fuller flavor.

About 75 cookies

  4 cups sifted flour
  1 teaspoon baking soda
  1 tablespoon ground cardamom
  1 tablespoon grated lemon rind
  1 tablespoon ground cinnamon
  ½ teaspoon ground cloves
  ½ teaspoon ground nutmeg
  ½ teaspoon freshly ground pepper
  ⅓ cup unsalted butter
  2 cups superfine sugar
  5 eggs
  2 tablespoons brandy (optional)
  2 cups coarsely ground mixed glacé fruit
  3 tablespoons hot milk
1½ cups sifted confectioners' sugar

Sift together the flour, baking soda, cardamom, lemon rind, cinnamon, cloves, nutmeg, and pepper. Cream the butter until soft and fluffy. Beat in the sugar, 2 tablespoons at a time, beating well after each addition. Beat in the eggs, one at a time, beating well after each addition. Beat in the brandy. Stir in the glacé fruit and mix well. Add the flour mixture to the batter and mix well; this is most easily done with your hands. Knead until the dough forms a ball. Cover with wax paper or plastic wrap and chill for 2 hours. Moisten your hands with cold water. Shape the dough into ¾-inch balls. Place on greased and floured baking sheets 2 inches apart. Let stand uncovered at room temperature overnight.

At baking time, preheat the oven to moderate (350° F).

Combine the milk and the confectioners' sugar to form a smooth paste. Brush as many balls as possible with the mixture and leave the other balls plain for contrast. Bake for about 15 minutes, or until golden brown at the edges.

MY FATHER'S FAVORITE GERMAN "S" COOKIES

Traditional Christmas cookies from my childhood, made as my mother made them.

About 40 cookies

½ cup unsalted butter
½ cup sugar
1 egg
2 egg yolks
1 teaspoon ground mace
1 teaspoon ground cardamom
2 cups sifted flour
¼ teaspoon baking powder

Cream the butter until soft and fluffy. Beat in the sugar, 2 tablespoons at a time, beating well after each addition. Beat in the whole egg and 1 egg yolk, and mix well. Stir in the mace and cardamom. Sift together the flour and baking powder, and gradually add it to the batter. With your hands, knead the dough until smooth. Wrap in wax paper or plastic wrap and chill for 1 hour. With your hands, roll the dough into sticks the thickness of a pencil. Tear off about 3 inches of the rolled dough and shape it into an "S" (or the shape of any other letter). Place cookies on buttered and floured baking sheets and let stand at room temperature for 2 hours.

At baking time, preheat the oven to moderate (350° F).

Beat the remaining egg yolk with 2 tablespoons water and brush each cookie with a little of the egg wash. Bake for 15 minutes or until just golden; do not brown.

Index